"No one sees the big picture of (leal. In *Kingdom Collaborators* he tells inspiring   al steps for how church, business, and social sector leaders can   ther for greater kingdom impact. If you are a leader with God-sized dreams and want to know how to make them happen, this book is for you!"
Dave Ferguson, lead pastor, Community Christian Church, Naperville, Illinois

"Some people just seem to always be a few steps ahead of the rest of us. Reggie is one of those people. I pay close attention to everything he writes. His themes are almost always a clear call to what's next, and this book is no exception."
Neil Cole, church planter, artist, author of *Organic Church* and *Church 3.0*

"Jesus began his ministry with slowly deconstructing what religion had become by painting a compelling picture of the reality of God's kingdom. With this as a starting point, Reggie deftly shows us who we need to be in order to reclaim that power and purpose that God had in mind for his world."
Nancy Ortberg, CEO, Transforming the Bay with Christ

"Reggie McNeal shares key characteristics and endeavors of effective Christian leaders who have chosen not to walk in well-worn footsteps but to pioneer transformative new paths in carrying out the Great Commission."
John Couch, vice president of education, Apple Inc.

"Reggie gives us permission to see the places and spaces we work and live as our mission field. At Gallup, we often write and speak about the impact of a leader's strengths and their ability to shape culture—the eight principles in this book give leaders the practical steps to do just that."
Jeremy Pietrocini, senior consultant, Gallup

"Reggie is an extraordinary friend and leader. He has the incredible ability to cast fresh vision on the work of the church in the world today, challenging Christian leaders to see collaboration as essential to being what Christ has called us to be. This book inspires all of us toward greater unity and commitment to Christ's transforming work."
Kevin Palau, president of Luis Palau Association, author of *Unlikely: Setting Aside Our Differences to Live Out the Gospel*

"Faith communities are critical partners with our city as we serve the growing needs in our community. Affordable housing, childcare, and literacy are just a few of the many areas in which the faith community can collaborate with local government to provide solutions. Once again, Reggie steps up and provides powerful, practical wisdom for leaders."

John D. Seybert, mayor of Redwood City, California

"Do you long to see broken lives restored? New life is the drive of *Kingdom Collaborators*. Reggie's passion for people is felt on every page, and he lives what he writes. He has helped us to birth a statewide coalition focused on awakening the faith-based community to bring hope to every child through serving our local schools. Be warned—reading *Kingdom Collaborators* may be hazardous to your comfortable life. It will change your status quo, muddy your hands, and free you from a predictable life!"

Lee Clamp, team leader for evangelism, South Carolina Baptist Convention

"Reggie has kingdom vision! For too long the church-as-institution has said 'come' but the Great Commission says 'go.' Reggie's charge in this book affirms, validates, and empowers kingdom leaders to recognize their circle of influence and to go turn this world upside down. This book is a must-read for all believers."

Joel D. Chapman, pediatrician, The Pediatric Clinic, Mt. Pleasant, Texas

"Millennials are largely disinterested in institutional religion, so church-based leadership models are increasingly passé. But few groups are more committed to making the world a better place than millennials. As such, they will resonate with the church-as-movement paradigm called for by Reggie McNeal. Seminaries need to pay attention. This book unfolds the exciting opportunity for pastors to calibrate their ministry as viral kingdom agents of human flourishing and is a call for leadership worthy of our unique moment in history."

John Seel, author of *The New Copernicans: Understanding the Millennial Contribution to the Church*

"Perhaps, for such a time as this, Jesus is changing our minds as it relates to understanding the call of all people. Perhaps now is the time that God is calling kingdom leaders to agitate for the kingdom, knowing that the agitation and advancement of God's kingdom is done with collective force and efforts. *Kingdom Collaborators* is the book to arrest your heart, expand your understanding, and prod you to move into God's calling no matter if you are clergy or congregant!"

Aleze M. Fulbright, director of leadership development, Indiana Conference of the United Methodist Church

"Using his personal observations, analyses, and interactions, Reggie McNeal has masterfully grasped leadership themes from those who are turning the world upside down. Reggie has written a must-read primer for anyone wanting to make a difference."

Henry Barton, vice president, government affairs, SCANA Corporation

"Kingdom collaboration is one of the most powerful, challenging, and beautiful enterprises possible. It requires honesty with one's self, faith in God's work through others, and perseverance when every barrier appears to stand against it. Reggie McNeal addresses these issues deeply steeped in the heart of Jesus with compassion for the challenge but urgency to press forward. Thank you, Reggie, for believing in us and cheering us on!"

Tracey Beal, executive director, School Connect, Glendale, Arizona

"The transformation of a community begins with the transformation of an individual. Whether one is a leader, collaborator, or follower, Reggie provides kingdom thinking to help unlearn traditions that are hindering our witness and work and relearn biblical principles that will unleash God's people. I believe this inspired book will help Christians join with God in his kingdom agenda, accelerating improvement on societal issues that is so desperately needed."

Susan Hewitt, executive director, UpWorks, St. Paul, Minnesota

"As a county judge, I routinely deal with individuals and families held captive by the dark kingdom, living far from life as God intends. I need help understanding my leadership role and learning how to promote the kingdom of God in my community. Dr. McNeal clarifies that responsibility and provides explanations, tools, and examples of kingdom leadership in today's world. Evangelism in 2017 most often begins with a compassionate helping hand extended by influential people who want to be a part of the change."

Brian Lee, county judge, Titus County, Mt. Pleasant, Texas

"*Kingdom Collaborators* continues the winsome and wise equipping mission of Reggie McNeal. But this book is much more than the sum of its brilliant analyses and insightful syntheses. *Kingdom Collaborators* is infused with the life of the kingdom—the breath of the Holy Spirit—from the first page until the last. The eight attributes, applicable stories, and concrete practices are a necessary wake-up call for a Western church often paralyzed by the hostility and indifference outside her walls. The insights are vital to majority world Christianity as well, with its challenges of making disciples that bridge Sunday's ecstasies and Monday's ethics. I was arrested by McNeal's unique combination of gracious and humble storytelling and prophetic confrontation with the status quo that compels both personal and community changes. I heartily recommend this book to all women and men of influence in all domains of society as they work to advance the justice, peace, and joy of the kingdom. These insights will be particularly helpful to church planters and local church revitalizers as they patiently labor for eternal impact."

Charlie Self, director of city development, Made to Flourish; professor of church history, Assemblies of God Theological Seminary

"*Kingdom Collaborators* is both a declaration of kingdom impact for the soul of the church and a call to eliminate the sacred and secular divide. Reggie McNeal has always been insightful; this book takes his keen insights and fashions them into a highly readable narrative. If you are a pastor, follower of Jesus, or someone who wants to make a difference in our world, this is your manifesto!"

John Jackson, president, William Jessup University

"I need a book like this to help me see the church and the world through the life-giving lens of the kingdom of God instead of the kingdom of the church. There is profound wisdom in these chapters that will inspire, bless, and challenge any church leader who reads it."

Herman R. Yoos, bishop, South Carolina synod, Evangelical Lutheran Church in America

"True leaders possess an internal passion to improve themselves for the sake of others. Imagine what could happen if you became such a leader. In *Kingdom Collaborators,* Reggie McNeal provides a fresh-cut path for anyone willing to increase their effectiveness. It's a journey worth taking because it will deliver what our world needs most: action."

David Staal, president and CEO, Kids Hope USA

"This book speaks of collaboration outside of the church walls and simply but strongly suggests that we can help drive the mission of Jesus through the work we do as Christians in our communities. As someone whose job intertwines a passion for education and a mission to serve, *Kingdom Collaborators* speaks to my heart."

Yolandé Anderson, director of family and community engagement, South Carolina Department of Education

REGGIE
McNEAL

KINGDOM
COLLABORATORS

EIGHT
SIGNATURE
PRACTICES
OF LEADERS
WHO TURN
THE WORLD
UPSIDE DOWN

IVP Books

An imprint of InterVarsity Press
Downers Grove, Illinois

InterVarsity Press
P.O. Box 1400, Downers Grove, IL 60515-1426
ivpress.com
email@ivpress.com

InterVarsity Press® is the book-publishing division of InterVarsity Christian Fellowship/USA®, a movement of students and faculty active on campus at hundreds of universities, colleges, and schools of nursing in the United States of America, and a member movement of the International Fellowship of Evangelical Students. For information about local and regional activities, visit intervarsity.org.

While any stories in this book are true, some names and identifying information may have been changed to protect the privacy of individuals.

Figures 1 and 2 are adapted from To Transform a City *by Eric Swanson and Sam Williams, Copyright © 2010 by Eric Swanson and Sam Williams. Used by permission of Zondervan. www.zondervan.com.*

Cover design: David Fassett
Interior design: Daniel van Loon
Images: © Mike Hill / Getty Images

ISBN 978-0-8308-4143-1 (print)
ISBN 978-0-8308-8536-7 (digital)

Printed in the United States of America ⊗

InterVarsity Press is committed to ecological stewardship and to the conservation of natural resources in all our operations. This book was printed using sustainably sourced paper.

Library of Congress Cataloging-in-Publication Data
A catalog record for this book is available from the Library of Congress.

P	23	22	21	20	19	18	17	16	15	14	13	12	11	10	9	8	7	6	5	4	3	2	1
Y	37	36	35	34	33	32	31	30	29	28	27	26	25	24	23	22	21	20	19	18			

To all kingdom leaders.

Thanks for turning the world right-side up

by turning it upside down!

THY KINGDOM

EVERYONE KNOWS that something big is up. The world is changing in ways that challenge every aspect of our lives, including our spiritual journeys. Not that long ago, people who were looking for God went to church to find him. There they assumed someone with superior spiritual understanding would tell them what to do. Teachers and church leaders provided instructions and activities to guide their development. These same leaders managed the church institution to make sure it marketed and delivered its spiritual goods and services to religious consumers. The size of the crowds and offerings on Sunday served as a public scorecard on the leaders' performance.

This fast-receding world demanded certain competencies of its leaders. They needed to be good Bible teachers (a love for studying ancient languages didn't hurt), able administrators, program developers, project managers, and soul-care experts who were politically savvy and able to demonstrate their command of parliamentary procedure. Those who experienced "the call to ministry" sought to master these skills with the clear expectation they would establish their ministry agenda in a church or church-related organization.

Fast-forward to today. Increasingly, people looking for meaning don't search for God at church on Sunday. They certainly don't think the church has a monopoly on the truth— spiritual or otherwise. Nor are they tempted to interrupt or change their life rhythms to become a church person to enhance their spiritual journey. They're just as likely to read a book (not necessarily one with a spiritual theme or written by a spiritual guide) or watch a movie, though they may discuss their spiritual interests with someone they respect.

So what kind of spiritual leader does *this* world demand? A different ilk of leader than the typical church-as-institution manager just described. The situation calls for *kingdom collaborators*. Those who are feeling the call to this leadership serve not only in church roles but also in jobs in every domain and sector in society (government, education, health care, the arts, business, the social sector, media, etc.). They evidence a signature set of competencies as they serve the church-as-movement, connecting God's work with people right where they live, work, play, go to school, work out, whatever. Kingdom collaborators have an affinity for community engagement and altruism and a love for God and neighbor that's both compelling and contagious. Because of their sense of call, they are intentional about both their life's meaning and their contribution. Underneath all this is their bedrock conviction that God is at work in every person in every situation in every area of life.

A powerful motivation drives these leaders. They hear the call to follow Jesus as a summons to focus on what he focused on: the kingdom of God. They believe that Jesus meant what he said when he taught us to pray "thy kingdom come." And they're looking for this kingdom to show up "on earth as it is in heaven." Viral kingdom leaders—leaders who infect those around them with their values—aren't just hoping for a better life in the hereafter; they're working to make it possible for people to enjoy a better life in the here-and-now. They see themselves as collaborators with God and others in answering this prayer.

Their perspective flows from their understanding of the kingdom. In their view, the kingdom can be characterized as *life as God intends*. Life *is* God's intent. There is *life* because God *is*. All life carries God's fingerprint because it emanates from him. It doesn't accidentally or randomly arise. Life has an intended purpose and quality because of God's will and character.

> VIRAL KINGDOM LEADERS AREN'T JUST HOPING FOR A BETTER LIFE IN THE HEREAFTER; THEY'RE WORKING TO MAKE IT POSSIBLE FOR PEOPLE TO ENJOY A BETTER LIFE IN THE HERE-AND-NOW.

The kingdom, Jesus taught, is the major work of God on planet Earth. God is busy in the world, reclaiming territory held captive by a usurping dark kingdom. This resurgence is the good news of the kingdom—and it is the gospel that Jesus proclaimed and lived out. He not only taught a kingdom message, he also lived the kingdom. He healed the sick, comforted the afflicted, and inspired hope for a better world. He embodied the life that God intends.

In contrast to Jesus' own robust life, the lives of most people seem to be a gross masquerade, a poor imitation of what God has in mind. So Jesus invites us into *his* life and clears the path for us through his passion, securing the better life by vanquishing sin, death, and the grave. His work on the cross and in the resurrection grant us full title to possess the life he offers. It's *real* life—life as God intends.

Accordingly, a kingdom perspective focuses on the quality of life for people in our communities—physical, economical, social, as well as spiritual. This understanding of the kingdom carries several implications. First, any church scorecard that doesn't extend to these dimensions of life doesn't accurately reflect Jesus' intentions for his church. I spent a lot of time making this case in my previous book (*Kingdom Come*), so I don't want to rehash that here. Unfortunately, the colossal misunderstanding of mission in the Western church has caused many institutional church leaders to regard lightly the work of their parishioners in other domains of culture (education, healthcare, business, arts, government, etc.). This view stems from how the church-as-institution sees its role relative to society. Figure 1 illustrates the typical institutional perspective.

The assumption underpinning this view is that, to have its greatest effectiveness, the church should concentrate on its own domain. This errant understanding means kingdom efforts may receive only scant attention at best or may not be recognized, encouraged, or even acknowledged by the institutional church. In too many cases, kingdom work is resisted by church-as-institution because it's viewed as activity that robs the church of vital resources it needs.

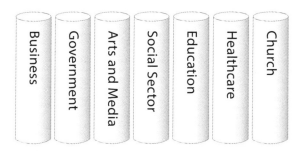

Figure 1. The church as institution

The reality is that most kingdom leaders operate largely outside the institutional church because they spend their lives in a wider bandwidth of human interest and activity. Embracing the church-as-movement paradigm recalibrates the church to be a people of God related to society as viral kingdom agents, positioned in every domain of culture. This thinking is illustrated in figure 2.

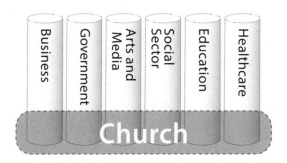

Figure 2. The church as movement

This shift reflects a kingdom narrative that acknowledges that God is at work in every domain of culture. Releasing and equipping the church to be the church where it is already deployed in the world—moving from the predominant church-as-institution perspective (church-centric thinking) to understanding church-as-movement (kingdom-centric thinking)—is the most critical challenge and opportunity for the church.

I'm not suggesting that past and current ecclesiology is unhelpful; I just think it needs a kingdom orientation. We need to regard the church through kingdom lenses, rather than looking at the kingdom through church-as-institution lenses. This is not the focus of this book, but it is a conviction that underpins it.

We need kingdom collaborators—kingdom leaders—to help navigate these new waters. (Throughout this book, the terms *kingdom leaders* and *kingdom collaborators* are used interchangeably.) Leaders who serve as apostles, prophets, teachers, pastors, and evangelists for the church-as-movement. Leaders who use their influence to work for people to experience the life God intends in every sphere and sector of society—from the board room to the classroom to the emergency room to the committee room to the workout room to the living room. In every cultural domain, in ways as distinct as the individual leaders involved, kingdom leaders must serve as co-conspirators with God to wreak havoc on the kingdom of anti-life.

While most kingdom leaders serve outside the church-as-institution, some kingdom leaders *can be* and *are* assigned to church-as-institution leadership roles. I'm happy to say that more and more leaders who hold positions with church-as-institution responsibilities are using their platforms to promote greater kingdom engagement by those who call themselves God's people. Most of my work involves these church leaders, many of whom are experiencing a spiritual rebirth as they pursue a more kingdom-centric ministry agenda. They are helping the church recover its missional integrity to point people to the kingdom. This is precisely what qualifies them as kingdom leaders.

Please don't hear what I am *not* saying. Church-as-institution serves a viable function in God's work on earth. The institutional church is the largest bundler of social capital in most communities. If this capital can be catalyzed and released into our communities, the church can be a part of moving the needle on big societal issues (those things that weigh in on whether people can experience life as God intends—such as education, economic development, and race relations). Most of the congregations and church groups I'm working with are figuring out ways to address one or more of these areas in their cities and neighborhoods. As this happens, the church becomes the agent of transformation so desperately needed across our country.

If you serve as a kingdom leader *outside* the church-as-institution, I hope this book affirms you as a significant player *in* the church-as-movement, whether or not you've ever served in a leadership capacity in the institutional church. You haven't come into your position of influence in your domain by accident. The King has strategically deployed you on purpose for a purpose. Your role in church-as-movement is no less valuable than serving as the leader of the largest congregation in your town or city.

I love what Michael Frost does in his weekly gathering of Jesus-followers in Sydney, Australia. According to him, the most treasured part of the worship experience is the ritual of calling out someone for "ordination." That person's gifts and talents are recited, his role in his everyday life is affirmed, and a prayer is offered commissioning him to kingdom service. The group lays on hands as part of the process. Frost declared, "I'm accused of trying to abolish the clergy. What I'm trying to do is to abolish the *laity*."

My reason for writing this book is to share some observations about the distinctive character and competencies of leaders who serve as kingdom collaborators. These insights come from the intersections I've had with kingdom leaders across a wide range of cultural engagement. These leaders demonstrate eight signature ways in which they operate—in their life and ministry across all sectors of society:

1. They practice a robust prayer life that helps them listen to and look for God.

2. They foment dissatisfaction with the status quo.

3. They combine social and spiritual entrepreneurship.

4. They marry vision with action.

5. They shape a people-development culture.

6. They curry curiosity.

7. They call the party in their city for collaborative initiatives.

8. They maintain an optimism amid the awareness that the kingdom has not yet fully come.

Each of these elements is treated in a chapter of their own in the pages that follow.

Writing this book is one way I'm praying "thy kingdom come." I dream that by focusing greater attention on kingdom leaders, we will get more of them. God knows we need them! Hopefully these pages will inspire, instruct, and release *you* to exercise your own collaboration to bridge heaven and earth.

Billy Graham is commonly quoted as having said this about Jesus' early followers: "The men who followed Him were unique in their generation. They turned the world upside down because their hearts had been turned right side up. The world has never been the same."

It's happening—again!

LIKE MANY PARENTS, Cathy and I routinely engaged our two daughters for prayer time as part of their bedtime ritual. Our younger daughter developed a habit of praying with her eyes open. One night I asked her why she did this. "Because I don't want to miss anything," she replied.

Kingdom leaders harbor the same desire. They've accepted God's invitation to join him in his kingdom mission, to become kingdom collaborators. Their efforts bridge heaven and earth. Kingdom collaborators believe God is at work in every person they encounter and in every situation they face. This means they stay on the lookout for what God is up to. They don't want to miss a thing!

How do kingdom leaders maintain this high God-alert status? This question brings us to the first and foundational element of eight signature practices that kingdom collaborators employ. These leaders believe that Jesus meant what he said when he instructed us to pray that God's kingdom would come on earth as it is in heaven. Accordingly, they *listen for* and *look for* God. These two dynamic engagements support God-conscious kingdom collaborators. They're learned attitudes and behaviors, not competencies relegated exclusively to a few from birth. Nor do these characteristics depend on some special spiritual dispensation. In other words, all of us can incorporate these practices into our thinking and living.

THESE LEADERS BELIEVE THAT JESUS MEANT WHAT HE SAID WHEN HE INSTRUCTED US TO PRAY THAT GOD'S KINGDOM WOULD COME ON EARTH AS IT IS IN HEAVEN.

In this chapter, we'll examine how our spiritual hearing and sight can be improved. Doing so will position us to be more effective collaborators with God in the kingdom that is unfolding all around us but can be missed if we aren't paying attention.

ARE WE TALKING *TO* OR TALKING *WITH* GOD?

Some years ago, I arranged to have dinner with a counselor friend of mine since I was going to be in his city on a speaking engagement. We met at a restaurant close to his office so he could come straight from work. As we sat down at our table, I asked him, "Well, how was your day?" Instead of the usual "Fine. How was yours?" he said, "I just finished a counseling appointment with a couple I've been seeing for a while. As we got started in the session, I asked them how it was going for them. For the next solid hour, all I got to say was 'I see,' 'Really?' and 'Hmm' as they talked nonstop. At the end of our session, they stood to leave and said, 'Thanks so much! We feel so much better now!'"

My friend went on with a chuckle, "It's like they upchucked all over me and just got up and walked out. I had plenty of feedback for them, but they never stopped talking long enough for me to get a word in edgewise! Oh well, they'll be back, and maybe I'll have a chance then." We both had a laugh and then settled into a discussion over the menu.

It hit me later that what my friend experienced was how I was treating God in my prayer life. "Dear God," would be followed typically by an "upchuck" of my life circumstances and needs. Once I finished updating God and offering him a few suggestions for how he could help me out, I'd wrap up the session "in Jesus' name" and rush off without giving him a chance to say a word.

God patiently waited a lot of years to get a word in edgewise with me. I grew up hearing the stories of prayer giants. George Mueller praying for milk and bread to feed the orphans in his care. Martin Luther quipping, "I've got so much to do today that I need to spend the first two hours in prayer." Billy Graham being caught prone and praying behind his desk. Perhaps all these stories are true, perhaps not. But I picked up one thing from being exposed to them: you need to pray a lot if you're going to do something big with God. But I confess, I often wondered why these great people of the faith needed to spend so much time with God. What was taking them so long to say what they had to say?

Boy, did I not get it! You see, in the spiritual tradition and tribe I grew up in, prayer was talking *to* God, not talking *with* God. We had formulas for working our way through prayer using categories of praise, confession, and thanksgiving, along with submitting requests (ACTS anyone?). Early in my writing career, my denomination asked me to write a set of lessons on prayer to serve as part of our Sunday school curriculum. I wrote thirteen weeks (a quarter's worth) of instruction on how to get the right stuff said and stuff said right when talking to God. Not one lesson I wrote raised the possibility that God may have something to say back to us. Sadly, no one noticed.

Talking *to* someone and talking *with* someone are two different dynamics. Only the latter employs the essentials of a genuine conversation. We've all been subjected to one-way verbal exchanges that left our need for conversation unmet. Either the other person talked nonstop without giving us a chance to say anything, or when we had the chance to speak, we knew she wasn't listening but was waiting for us to come up for air so she could take over again. In such cases, I typically lose patience and give up trying to have a conversation.

I'm afraid I've been guilty of both violations in my prayer life. Thankfully, God has much more patience than I do. He hangs in there, hoping I'll give him a chance to speak into my life.

Some years ago, I started listening more in prayer in case God has something to say to me. Turns out, he has plenty! I listen because there's no voice like his. His words penetrate to the core of my being, bringing calm, courage, correction, and confirmation like no one else or no other words can do. God sometimes uses Scripture to remind me of a truth he has already spoken. In other instances, he reminds me of things that people have said or brings to mind the words of a hymn or song or something I've read. God also uses images to communicate. These may include memories of events and encounters that have something to contribute to the current conversation. They can also involve metaphors that help me picture God in our exchange (like a father, counselor, friend).

All these communications not only take aim at my rational mind; they often address my emotions, providing information and instruction for my soul that transcend words, touching my spirit, aligning my thoughts with his.

A few years ago I met with a few dozen church leaders in Portugal. The group represented a dozen European countries. One woman from a former Soviet country asked if she could share something with me to get my comments. I had become quite impressed with how this woman, high up in the government of her country, unapologetically displayed her Christian faith (quite a remarkable turnaround from Soviet days), so I was eager to hear what she had to say.

She took a piece of paper out of her purse that had a drawing on it. "I received this image from God in a dream," she said. "I don't quite know what it means, but I think it is a clue as to how I am to proceed with a national ministry of prayer." I told her that she had drawn a network system that was simple (but sophisticated) that would allow her to replicate her national prayer event (held in the capitol) in every region of her country if she built and staffed the system. She began to cry as we talked, telling me this very idea had been her vision for several years, but she had been unclear as to how to proceed. God had answered her in a dream with a network diagram! He loves to come to the aid of his kingdom leaders.

Other voices inside our heads also clamor for attention. Our self-talk channel runs 24-7, drawing from all kinds of sources: family, friends, critics, supporters, and what's transpiring around us, just to name a few. Some of these inputs are audio recordings that we play from our past—from people in our family of origin to significant people in our lives who have helped to shape our personal narrative (more about this later). And, without fail, the enemy of our soul also maintains an active channel where he pumps fear, confusion, doubt, guilt—all designed to create static so we don't hear the voice of calm, assurance, truth, love.

With all these competing voices in our head, how do we recognize the voice of God? We can always be sure that he speaks truth, so anything that doesn't square with his work is not from him. Also, his words always line up with his character. He doesn't say one thing and do another. His instruction and insight typically serve to heighten our relationship with and trust in him.

How do we put ourselves in a position to hear God's voice in our prayer life? We help ourselves to hear God by *expecting* to hear God. He won't usually force himself on us, but he wants to talk with us, so he patiently waits for our willingness to open up lines of communication. Our predisposition to obedience—an attitude of saying yes to what he says—also plays a big role in promoting a high-def signal.

Having said all this, know that hearing God requires practice. I think it was Luther who said, "There is one Voice that I have learned to hear above all others." Learning takes time and involves mistakes. We won't always get it right. But we can be sure that God wants to be in conversation with us, so don't worry that your mishears will scare him off. Keep at it, striving to hear his voice. Jesus offered his encouragement to us, saying, "My sheep listen to my voice; I know them" (John 10:27).

WHAT'S YOUR POSITION ON PRAYER?

This question isn't about our physical posture when we're in prayer (bowed head, kneeling, standing, prostrate—they all have their times). I'm thinking more about our perspective on the position we think we're in as we engage God.

An insight came to me as I listened to a professional executive coach make a presentation about what he called "the three levels of coaching." The first level, he said, involves identifying the problem. In this phase, the coach helps the client articulate the issue he or she wants to focus on. This clarification often helps the client move beyond the presenting problem to identify the real issues that are creating the dilemma. The coach then described the second level of coaching, where the coach assists the client in developing strategies for addressing the problem he or she has identified.

Then the coach began describing the third level of coaching. He commented that this level was more challenging than the first two, and rarely did the coaching make it to that level. He called this arena "the level of identity." In this phase, the coach helps the client deal with self-perceptions and personal elements that impact their situation. These discussions help the clients understand what *they* are contributing to the problems they face. What are their fears, for example?

Who are they unwilling to disappoint? Any number of issues can surface during this exploration. The coach also guides clients to claim the strengths they bring to the situation, helping them own the talent and expertise they possess that they can draw on to confront their situation.

As I heard this coach describe these levels that he moved through with his clients, I suddenly realized that he was describing various levels, or dynamics, of praying. This description actually captured the position many of us adopt as we communicate with God in prayer. Often we identify the problem to God as we see it ("Lord, I've got a problem," followed by a summary of the situation). Next we outline several strategies he should consider in dealing with this ("would you just," followed by our best ideas of what needs to be done or what outcome needs to be realized). We then punctuate our prayer with a fervent plea that he would hurry up and do something; or, if he can't work on it right then, that he would help us have patience to wait it out.

But Jesus didn't pray this way at all. He had a very different approach. He prayed from his position of identity—as a son talking with his dad. He didn't dwell on clarifying problems or identifying strategies for the Father. His petitions were borne out of his relationship with God, not pled as a beggar or as a desperately hopeful player of the prayer lottery.

Nowhere was this more clearly demonstrated than in his last hours, when he was in the throes of his passion. In his high priestly prayer, he began his conversation in Gethsemane with "Father, the hour has come. Glorify your Son, that your Son may glorify you" (John 17:1). Later, on the cross and with his last breath, he shouted, "Father, into your hand I commit my spirit" (Luke 23:46). The Son was always in conversation with his Father.

Jesus taught his disciples to do the same. When they asked him to teach them to pray, it wasn't as if they had never prayed before. It's just that they had never prayed like *he* prayed. So he gave them the biggest lesson up front by telling them to open their prayers with "Our Father" (Matthew 6:9). These are words that reveal a relationship, that reveal *our* identity. We are God's children. This is the position we hold. This perspective colors everything about our conversations with him.

I can take the typical approach in my prayer life of updating God on my finances (or whatever) and asking him to help if he wants to (I know he can). Or I can take the position of a son and say, "Father, I want to thank you for always meeting my needs. I look forward to being amazed at how you are already moving to make provision again. Your constant provision helps me love you even more." What a difference this kind of praying makes! Anxiety over my problems gives way to celebration and confidence as I speak as God's son. Prayer becomes a reminder of my identity. It moves from being merely a session to launder requests before God to a venue where identities are nurtured and bolstered.

WHAT TIME DO YOU PRAY?

God engages us from our future.

We all have had experiences of learning something just before we needed to know it or meeting someone in the "nick of time" who became vital to our next assignment. Are these coincidences? Hardly! God is operating in our lives from where we are headed—what we call our future. He is the ultimate begin-with-the-end-in-mind guy! Since he knows where we're headed, he shepherds us along our paths and dials into our life so we experience exactly what we need for our next chapter.

We tend to think that our past prepares us for the future, because that's how we experience it. The reality is the other way around: future challenges inform today's preparation so we can meet them. This makes God the ultimate trusted source for helping us understand what to do right now, because only he has worked through our future. His instructions are so that we can be better prepared for what's headed our way.

This perspective provides us another motivation for listening to God. And it also changes the way we listen. For much of my life, my prayers involved updating God, bringing him up to speed on what was happening in my life so I could ask for his help. Now I know that prayer is God's gift to me for updating *me* on what's happening, for bringing *me* up to speed, for helping *me* see what *he* is up to.

The understanding of time that has emerged in quantum theory helps us understand this perspective. In Newtonian physics, time is a constant. Not so in a quantum world. Past, present, and future are all parts of the same reality. The future is incipient in the present; the past gives meaning to the present; one can't be severed from the other. Though our experience is that we move from the past toward the future, it's just as accurate to say that the future is hurtling toward us.

At whatever point God intersects time, the impact reaches across all time. The declaration of God that "I am the Alpha and Omega . . . who is, and who was, and who is to come" (Revelation 1:8) is not just an allegory, but can be contemplated as reality in a quantum universe. The work of Jesus on the cross—his "it is finished"—counted for *all* time. While this event occurred in history, it's also possible to talk of the Lamb slain "from the creation of the world" (Revelation 13:8). The cross event displays how the future impacts the meaning of events.

Lots of people died on crosses in the Roman world. What made Jesus' death significant was the cross's silhouette against the future empty tomb. The resurrection secured the efficacy of Jesus' sacrifice. The empty tomb announced the future of sin and death.

The kingdom is a future that's always invading the present. Every expression of good, of victory over evil, of transcendent beauty, points us forward to the kingdom. Every aspiration of hope is an echo of a preferred future pressing into today's world. When worship transports us to a sense of timelessness or when we celebrate the death of saints (anticipation has turned to reality for them), these experiences point us to the future-breaking-into-the-present kingdom.

THE KINGDOM IS A FUTURE THAT'S ALWAYS INVADING THE PRESENT.

Haven't you had the experience of thinking about a person only to run into or hear from him shortly thereafter? Or perhaps you've called someone who starts a phone conversation with "Have your ears been burning?" or tells you that you had been on her mind. These seemingly random and sometimes mysterious occurrences point us to one significant reality of quantum spirituality: our inner being can vibrate and resonate—pick up signals—from what's happening across space and time.

In one of his famous miracles, Jesus pointed to the dynamic I'm describing. The cursing of the fig tree (Matthew 21:18-20; Mark 11:12-14, 20-21) actually involved a fast-forwarding of the future. The tree in the episode was dying—made plain by Mark's reference to the fact that it wasn't the time of year for figs (in fact, it also wasn't the time of year for leaves). The tree was seriously and obviously out of round, "acting out" with its display of leaves with no accompanying fruit. It was in the early throes of death.

Jesus merely called the future into the present. What did his disciples remark about this episode? Not "you killed that fig tree!" but "how did the fig tree wither so quickly?" (Matthew 21:20). And they observed that the tree had withered from its roots (Mark 11:20), an indication of the inevitability of the tree's death, just fast-forwarded by Jesus.

In both Matthew and Mark, this episode immediately led into a discussion of prayer. Jesus told them that in prayer we have the ability to hurry along the future (mountains falling into the sea was activity associated with eschatological visions of the end of time). If the whole encounter had been about judging a tree for not having fruit (when it shouldn't have anyway), the teaching on prayer would make little sense.

However, if the incident demonstrates the power of God to bring future realities into the present, the teaching on prayer helps us grasp its meaning and power as a kingdom activity. If we can capture what God wants to do in a situation, what outcome he would prefer, how he is working, our agreement with him in our praying releases the power to align the present with the preferred future.

Jesus demonstrated the power of this perspective in his great high priestly prayer in John 17. He reminisced about the future in order to draw strength for his passion: "And now, Father, glorify me in your presence with the glory I had with you before the world began" (John 17:5). Past, present, and future all became one as Jesus thought about where he was headed. Recalling that destination gave him what he needed to face what we can't even imagine. And because he found what he needed to get through it, the kingdom of God triumphed over the usurper kingdom that had diminished life as God intends.

Recalling Jesus' experience provides even greater incentive for us to engage in prayer more—but not in a manner that rehearses the past. The perspective I'm talking about gives us a much more robust prayer life. In the Sermon on the Mount, Jesus instructed his disciples not to babble like pagans in prayer—"for your Father knows what you need before you ask him"—but to get straight to fast-forwarding the future: "Your kingdom come, your will be done on earth as it is in heaven" (Matthew 6:8, 10).

I can't recount the number of times I've received a heads-up from the Spirit while in a listening mode. The most significant was a week when I felt in my spirit that there was a gathering storm, a leadership challenge headed my way in the ministry assignment I held. Over a period of days, the size and shape of the challenge became clearer. By the time it emerged from underground meetings to create a public crisis, I had been steeled for the encounter. The voice of God to me was both direct and mediated through a series of un-solicited notes I received from prayer warriors sharing their strong impulses and pointing me to specific Scripture pas-sages that had been impressed on them. The whole sad tale was the most excruciating leadership episode of my life, but also one of the most robust periods of prayer I've experienced.

I'm not a mystic or clairvoyant. I claim no special unction or gift. And those who know me would certainly tell you I don't possess a spiritual prowess that sets me up for hearing from God. I've just learned to listen. His thoughts and in-sights are promised to us all (James 1:5); it's just a matter of tuning in.

Listening to God in our prayer life helps us be better sit-uated for our challenges as kingdom leaders. It attunes us to the future God wants us to have. If we listen to God in prayer, he can help us catch up to what he's doing. Kingdom leaders consciously or intuitively have figured this out.

WHAT'S NEW WITH YOU?

Kingdom collaborators hear from God because they've learned to *listen*. But they've also learned to *look* for God. They see him everywhere and in every situation, especially in the lives of people around them. God sightings are more common for those who intentionally practice looking and who learn how God most often shows up.

I often suggest to people that, when looking for God, they should look at the *new* things going on in their lives. That new challenge, new opportunity, new problem, new relationship, new whatever, is most likely where God is at work. Why do I say this? Because I believe God prefers new.

We don't automatically associate new with God. Most people think of God as old. I understand why. He's been around a long time, and Sistine Chapel depictions and other artists' renderings typically show him with a long, white beard. But a timeless being doesn't age. God simply *is*. Artists could just as easily paint him as someone in his strapping youth. There's no real damage here one way or the other, except that the perception that God is old can get in our way of seeing him. It can cloud our thinking. When we think of him as old, we tend to think of him as if he lives in the past and is threatened by having to cope with new challenges just like we are.

This perception can cause us to think that God has been painted into a corner with our situations and is striving to overcome challenges and circumstances he didn't anticipate. We can find ourselves praying to a God who needs our help in strategizing and implementing solutions. We wind up using prayer to inform God rather than to be informed by him.

From Genesis to Revelation, "new" is the take on God. The creation of the universe was new when it happened, as was each order of design and being—especially human beings, who uniquely are made in the image of God. The God who declares, "See, I am doing a new thing" (Isaiah 43:19), doesn't cease his creative activity once the book of beginnings comes to a close.

The Old Testament is full of new activity on God's part. He even does some repeat acts in new ways. For instance, when Moses led the liberated slaves out of Egypt, their first stop was the Red Sea. At a seeming dead end, God made passage for them to walk on dry ground through water stacked up on both sides so they could escape the pursuing Egyptians.

A generation later, the Israelites would enter the Promised Land through another dry crossing. This time God accomplished the feat through a different approach. He dammed up the river miles upstream, only commencing the process when the priests led the way by putting their feet in the water. It took some time for the river to run dry; those priests had to be sopping wet—and relieved— by the time the water receded.

Why would God pull off a dry-ground crossing in two different ways? I think one answer is that every generation needs its own dry-ground crossing. Those entering Canaan needed a different story to tell than an old dramatic episode. So do we! We need to see God act in our own day and time in ways that make sense in our current reality. The challenge to do this doesn't intimidate him. In fact, he has set it up this way! A totally predictable God would leave very little room for faith. And, the Scripture says, without faith it is *impossible* to please God (Hebrews 11:6). So God keeps sending new things our way to build our faith muscles as we respond to fresh challenges and opportunities. He also sends new mercies. Anyone want old manna?

The New Testament offers many other glimpses into the preference of God to be at work in new ways. The incarnation and Pentecost certainly sit at the top of the list of examples. Others include Jesus instructing his disciples with a new command and a new covenant (John 13:34; Mark 14:24). We are *new* creatures in Christ, the apostle Paul said (2 Corinthians 5:17). And John on Patmos tells us we're headed to a new heaven, where we will receive not only new resurrection bodies but a new wardrobe (Revelation 3:4) and new names (Revelation 2:17). And in a moment tying the end of the Bible to the beginning, God declared, "I am making everything new" (Revelation 21:5).

Adopting the perspective that God is at work in the new does something inside us. It builds faith, but it also does something beyond us. It allows us to become voices of hope and opportunity in our communities. Most people look at what they see as intractable problems—issues like generational poverty and homelessness—and wonder if things can ever be any different or better. Kingdom leaders, on the other hand, look at the same situations and see new options— because they see *God* at work. While others wring their hands in the face of daunting challenges, kingdom collaborators are busy helping people experience the life God intends for them. They are demonstrating kingdom leadership.

Throughout this book, you'll hear stories of some of these leaders and the remarkable work they're doing. They are captured and motivated by the vision of a better world. They see people enjoying better lives in every arena: spiritual, educational, health, financial, relational—all the ways that people pursue life. They also see better communities that support life as God intends. Their vision compels them to collaborate with God and others to work for their vision to become reality. They lead with confidence, because they see God.

The kingdom of God is an unfolding reality, informed by a sure and certain future. We know how it all ends. The kingdom *will* come. We need leaders who participate in and help us experience the kingdom now—on earth as it is in heaven. They accomplish this by listening for and looking for God. These leaders' prayer lives support their efforts as they collaborate with God and others to bridge heaven and earth.

It's been decades now since Cathy and I prayed with our girls when they climbed into bed at night. But the lesson I learned one of those nights still resonates with truth. We should be careful not to miss God at work in his kingdom around us. He has invited us to collaborate with him in his great redemptive mission.

Kingdom collaborators pray with their eyes wide open!

ALASKA

RYAN PICKED HIS MOMENT. He had been asked to speak at the local ministers' monthly prayer breakfast. During the two years since an initial meeting, the gathering had blossomed from a small group to dozens of regular attenders. The participants' conversations over the months had built a solid network of fellowship, reversing decades of dissociation among the community's spiritual leaders.

But for some time, Ryan had been experiencing a growing conviction that the group needed to move beyond fellowship as its goal. Specifically he wanted to see the group adopt and pursue an epic win that would improve the lives of people in their city.

Customarily the speaker would bring a "word of encouragement" to the group. Ryan chose a different tack. He began with an uncomfortable question: "Why does any kid get out of our city's schools unable to read when our congregations are full of people who can?" He then mounted a passionate plea for the assembled spiritual leaders to seek the welfare of the city as their top priority, using the message of the prophet Jeremiah as his text (Jeremiah 29:4-7). His opening question drove home the point that the church in the city could and should collaborate to address societal ills. Ryan's message and choice of moment makes perfect sense to kingdom leaders.

Recently the insurance company GEICO has run a series of television commercials using a similar script with an identical tag line. Each ad's plot goes like this: "If you are a _____ (skater, actor, etc.), you _____ (fill in the blank with an activity that goes with the role). It's what you do!" If you're a kingdom leader, you agitate for the kingdom. It's what you do. Kingdom leaders agitate by fomenting dissatisfaction with the status quo.

King, Lincoln, Luther, Mandela—these well-known leaders fomented dissatisfaction with the status quo of their day in hopes of creating a better world. I know other kingdom leaders—Lewis, Barton, Hubert, Gaddini—who aren't famous but are stubbornly convinced that God has something better for their communities. They're willing to agitate for their cause.

Very little progress in our world happens without disruption. Sometimes shifts are small and localized; sometimes they impact an entire culture. When we consider disruptive forces, we almost always think about technological advances that render previous technology less desirable or obsolete. DVDs replaced VHS tapes for movie viewing; cassette tapes

VERY LITTLE PROGRESS IN OUR WORLD HAPPENS WITHOUT DISRUPTION.

gave way to CDs, which in turn yielded to downloadable iTunes. Email's ascendency created the term *snail mail*, which refers to what previously had been the norm (written correspondence).

This disruptive dynamic is at work in every societal sphere. Online learning challenges the conventional residential college approach to adult education. Hospitals buy up physicians' practices, and new medical discoveries replace previously preferred treatments. In the spiritual domain, leaders and institutions struggle with the implications that fewer and fewer people are susceptible to being congregationalized. The idea that the search for God-connection can be relegated to a particular set of activities at certain places on prescribed days seems increasingly quaint, a throwback to a time when people had to go to the theater to see movies or shop at a music shop to buy records.

Kingdom leaders grasp the need for disruption to move us closer to the life God intends. History supports their view. Slavery in the United States didn't go down without a fight (actually, it took a war). Discrimination and injustice don't naturally abate. Rather, it takes contentious debate, hard-fought court cases, and legislative battles to confront and to stop them. The overhaul of the healthcare system won't come without the pain of failure to precipitate a crisis that will generate spirited political debate and the exercise of

KINGDOM LEADERS GRASP THE NEED FOR DISRUPTION TO MOVE US CLOSER TO THE LIFE GOD INTENDS.

political will. Even spiritual leaders recognize that spiritual renewal requires repentance, a disruption evidenced by a change of direction.

This chapter focuses on the art of agitation as a tool of choice in the kingdom leader's toolkit. I'm not talking about change for change's sake. The change that kingdom leaders seek is change that unlocks the treasures of God's kingdom for life here on earth.

First let me offer a qualifying and clarifying word. Just because kingdom leaders tend to incite disgruntlement doesn't mean they, themselves, are unlikeable or unpleasant. Kingdom leaders aren't merely contrarians, though they espouse a contrarian perspective that calls for significant societal and cultural transformation. They foment for a strategic purpose. They agitate for the kingdom.

The well-known leaders I mentioned above—famous for the challenges they posed to the existing world order—weren't unlikeable or deficient in relational capacity. They didn't agitate because their Myers-Briggs Type Indicator was J-E-R-K.

Nelson Mandela serves as an example of what I'm talking about. On a recent trip to Johannesburg, South Africa, I toured the Soweto Township where Mandela's home and the Apartheid Museum are located. I also visited the Robben Island prison facility (now a museum) off the coast of Cape Town, where Mandela was imprisoned for years for his anti-apartheid views. The portrait of Mandela that emerges from an immersion into his life is that of a gregarious, affable, even charming person whose relational bandwidth stretched from the poor of the township populations to the academic and political elite of the world.

Kingdom leaders who agitate for a better world are in good company. Even the most cursory understanding of Jesus' ministry picks up on the fact that he was a rabble-rouser. He agitated against the prevailing religious authorities of his day, calling them hypocrites, vipers, and children of the devil. He railed against the spiritual devastation that these so-called spiritual leaders caused, placing unfair and consternating burdens on people that complicated their lives and did nothing for their spiritual development except to get in the way of it.

Jesus challenged such leaders not just for their errant theology, but also for their self-serving motives. He used his last public utterance to issue a blistering indictment of the scribes and Pharisees (Matthew 23). Rabbi Jesus had serious issues with his religious contemporaries!

How do kingdom leaders foment strategically to create energy for overcoming the inertia of status-quo conditions that need kingdom intervention? What are some key insights and elements that kingdom leaders employ to stir people to action? Five things come to mind.

1. AGITATE BY SELLING THE PROBLEM

Leaders are supposed to offer solutions to correct problems, right? Yes, but when it comes to introducing and managing significant change, they first need to "sell the problem." Leaders can rush too quickly to solve problems that haven't been fully articulated. When they prematurely assume that people understand why they're proposing change, they raise the risk that the change will be resisted. If followers don't understand the problem the leader is trying to solve, they fail to embrace whatever solution the leader proposes.

When experiencing rejection of this sort, the leader may wrongly conclude that her idea was rebuffed, when in fact it just didn't make sense to her followers. "If it ain't broke, don't fix it" is not just a witticism; it's the way many people think. The leader's task in leading significant change often starts with crafting a compelling narrative to inform people that something is broken and why it needs fixing.

Effective kingdom leaders don't risk failure at this point. They want people to understand the nature of whatever issue they want them to engage in. Once people understand why something is a problem, they're more likely to embrace an effort to address it. Simon Sinek, a business consultant, says it this way in his TED talk: "People don't buy *what* you do; they buy *why* you do it." He suggests that, in the end, people follow leaders for their own sake, because they believe that the leader believes what they do. They have, in essence, adopted the leader's *why* as their own.

A leader articulates a problem. This can be and often is very effective, particularly if the leader enjoys favor with her followers. Denise Holland, executive director of the Harvest Hope Food Bank in my city (Columbia, South Carolina), has done a masterful job selling a huge problem. Denise knows that "hunger" as a problem is impersonal and not very compelling. So she works hard putting a face on hunger. She tells stories of people visiting the food bank, showing up desperate and leaving with hope as well as food. Denise tells you how many meals ten dollars will buy for a family of four. But she also scales the problem to touch the hearts and pocketbooks of donors who can contribute much larger sums.

It takes tons of food to serve the multiple counties that comprise what we call the Midlands of South Carolina. Denise can rattle off exactly how many tons and dollars! In short, she has sold the problem. As a result, people and businesses, churches and schools, neighborhoods and banks continue to respond to her food-raising and fundraising efforts.

But the leader doesn't necessarily have to be the one to sell the problem. Sometimes another voice can be more effective. Pastor Lynne crafted a one-two punch using this rationale. First she arranged for me to spend three hours on a Saturday morning with her key congregational leaders. Her assignment to me was to share what making the kingdom a priority (as we're commanded by Jesus) would mean in terms of the church's ministry agenda. She asked me to give plenty of examples of how churches were engaging their communities and changing their scorecards for ministry effectiveness, including some of their community work. That I did, and the leaders were seemingly embracing the notions I shared.

But the wise pastor left nothing to chance. At lunch she brought in the principal of the Title 1 elementary school less than a mile from the church. This energetic young principal took questions from the crowd about the challenges she faced in her assignment and what kind of help she needed. The response to her was nothing short of amazing. On the spot, people volunteered left and right to meet many of the needs, from mentoring kids to helping teachers move into and decorate their classrooms to planting flowerbeds. The pastor's smart strategy paid off in the high degree of personal response by the congregational leaders and the formation of a relationship with that school that benefited teachers, students, and administrators. Oh, and it did wonders for the church as well.

I routinely recommend to church leaders that they interview community leaders as part of their gatherings every month or so. Police chiefs, hospital administrators, social workers, city council members, county officials—all can be tremendous allies in problem *selling* to pave the way to problem *solving.* Sometimes these people are members of the church but have never been asked to address their fellow church members about their community roles and responsibilities, as well as the challenges they face or the needs they have.

Last week, when I made this suggestion to a group of pastors, one of them told me afterward, "I have two elementary school principals in my congregation. I can't believe I've never asked them what they could use from us! I'm going to put both of them up in front of our people." That pastor passed on to me an email from one of those principals expressing how honored she would be to have the chance to share with their congregation some of her daily challenges. I predict that when this happens (it's scheduled soon), the congregation is going to have bigger (and better) problems to tackle than it had before.

2. AGITATE BY REFRAMING AND FLIPPING (NARRATIVES, NOT HOUSES)

Often a leader's quest to foment dissatisfaction with the status quo involves two different but related approaches. One requires helping other people see or understand the problem that the leader sees through restating the problem or question she's trying to address. After all, in-the-box questions get in-the-box answers.

Sometimes an issue needs a new expression that involves looking at it from another angle. We call this process "reframing." The second approach involves creating new, often surprising solutions that challenge status-quo responses to the problem. This development inspires hope that the problem can be solved, which motivates people to become involved in the solution. In effect, those involve "flipping the script": creating new solution narratives that reflect and allow new approaches to old problems. Both practices—reframing and flipping—can accelerate healthy engagement around some issue that needs to be addressed.

Reframing. Rick called me this morning. He has developed a successful counseling practice, including a large clientele of churchgoers and clergy. One of Rick's specialties is helping couples that struggle with sexual intimacy. He has helped hundreds of clients work through this very delicate aspect of their marriage with very positive outcomes. He called to tell me that he would like to help dozens of couples simultaneously through marriage retreats and seminars rather than helping only one couple at a time in counseling sessions.

Rick has contacted pastors with his offer of service but is getting very little positive response, even though pastors know this is a big problem for many of their congregants. Rick's dilemma involves helping pastors get dissatisfied with the status quo of couples enduring intimacy-deficit marriages.

I suggested to Rick that he reframe his offer. Rather than offering help for congregants' marriages, he would begin to offer help to *the pastors*. His narrative would be built around a felt need of spiritual leaders by pointing out how he can offer some help to *them*. Rick's new approach involves questions like "Have you ever wished you could escape those embarrassing conversations with people about their sex lives?" or "Would you like to know what to say the next time a couple talks to you about their sexual intimacy?" or even "Would you like to reduce your counseling load?" Rick will garner greater receptivity to his offer through this reframing of the problem. Rather than increasing the tension by focusing on the same old problem, sometimes the way to increase dissatisfaction to the point of action involves coming through another door, reframing the issue in another narrative.

Flipping the script. I first ran into this term when I read an article describing a development in the field of education. In the standard instructional model, a teacher introduces concepts in a classroom and then sends students home to practice the new element (like working math problems) or to process the information they've received (through additional reading or a paper to write). The idea is that homework helps students apply what they learn in the classroom.

Some innovative schools have flipped this script. Instruction has moved away from the classroom to online access, making instruction available anywhere and repeatable for greater comprehension. Homework then takes place in the classroom, where the teacher can provide assistance and even one-on-one attention to a student struggling to apply new knowledge, for example. Learning approaches can be customized to the student's own learning style, allowing for group settings, individual practice, project application—whatever helps the learner consolidate her learning. Talk about flipping the script!

But some people are at work changing the narrative of an entire community. I ran into one of these stories a couple of years ago when I met Scott Sheppard, the executive director of 6 Stones ministry in Euless, Texas (6Stones.org). In 2008, Scott was serving as the missions pastor at First Baptist Church of Euless, watching their middle-class bedroom community of Dallas transform into an ethnically and economically diverse city (with 119 nations represented, speaking seventy languages). Increasingly people were facing economic challenges on multiple fronts, from dilapidated housing to food insecurity.

That year, the church made a courageous, script-flipping decision. Instead of seeing missions as only overseas involvement, they decided to adopt a kingdom narrative of addressing their city's needs by creating an organization designed to be a coalition of churches, businesses, and other nonprofit agencies to become a one-stop shop for addressing community needs. The church recommissioned Scott to serve as the executive pastor of the new organization (also called 6 Stones) with a starting allocation of $200,000. They repurposed a church facility across the street (an old strip mall) into offices and a warehouse for the new organization. Their first major project involved garnering 150 volunteers to renovate eighteen homes to make them livable spaces.

What has transpired over the past eight years is nothing short of miraculous. Here are just *some* of the results: The coalition now has over a dozen business partners and 76 participating congregations. To date, 541 homeowners have had their homes repaired to code in an annual project called CPR (Community Powered Regeneration). Over $9 million have been invested in the community. Over a quarter million volunteer hours have helped 106,489 individuals with a variety of services, including providing backpacks of school supplies for 26,720 kids and Christmas gifts for 22,659 kids at their annual "Night of Hope" events held at all ten of the school district's elementary schools. (The local school district serves as a wildly enthusiastic champion because of all the help received from 6 Stones.) The giving to the organization has increased nine-fold, from the initial allocation to over $1.8 million in 2016.

Early on, the ministry made the decision that it would share the gospel in word as well as deed, so everyone who receives help also hears about Jesus (not as a prerequisite for receiving help). Hundreds of people have decided to become Jesus-followers, and many now work as volunteers in the ministry.

I love this script-flipping quote that Scott often repeats when telling the story of 6 Stones. "It's amazing what you can do if you don't know you shouldn't do it." What began as discontentment with watching the deterioration of the city has turned into successful community revitalization. That's what kingdom leaders do.

3. AGITATE WITH POLITICAL SAVVY

In his book *Leading Change*, Harvard business professor John Kotter discusses eight steps involved in successfully transforming organizations. One of his recommendations is that the change leader build a powerful guiding coalition to ensure the success of whatever change and transition needs to take place. Both parts of that descriptive phrase are important: the coalition needs to be composed of powerful people—people whose public support usually means the cause is adopted and accomplished, and people who can help to guide the change and transition. These coalition members aren't puppets; they're used to having significant input, and what they have to say is worth listening to by the leader. They help to shape both strategy and implementation. By gaining such buy-in from these people, the leader stands a much greater chance of having a successful outcome.

Achieving this dynamic or employing this strategy effectively often requires the leader to be politically savvy— knowing the right people to agitate to get something done. Significant change often requires influential people to put some muscle into the effort, particularly if the issue is an entrenched one. Nehemiah serves as a great Old Testament example of both of these truths playing out. He used his position and relationship with the king to position himself with resources and authority to address the rebuilding of Jerusalem. Once on the ground there, he had to deal with the local leaders of the remnant population as well as with the hostile forces of Sanballat. He performed brilliantly on all fronts.

Being politically savvy doesn't mean being sleazy or crooked or disingenuous. Politics is the art of getting people with disparate agendas to work together to achieve common goals. Too bad *politics* has become a dirty word. This reflects more on the character of the people involved than on the concept itself. Effective leaders excel in pulling people together to achieve something they determine is worth doing. Either instinctively or through learned behavior, kingdom leaders know how to make the "right" people agitated—and then listen to them.

I'm working with a young and savvy leader right now in a statewide literacy effort. The epic win he has identified involves every school in our state having some kind of church sponsorship (supplying readers, putting together weekend backpacks with food, providing various forms of teacher support). He has been agitating for almost two years, using his position of leadership in a denominational role to convene groups of church leaders for one-day gatherings. At this event, he introduces them to kingdom thinking and makes the case for school engagement.

All along, Lee has been building a relationship with the state superintendent of education and her office, including an appointee who is tasked specifically to work with the faith community to generate school engagement. He has also put together a cross-domain steering group with powerful con-nections, which acts as a guiding coalition.

Lee's patience is paying off. Reports are beginning to roll in of local initiatives underway as church leaders catch a vision for what they can do and *why* they need to do it. There's more to come! Solutions are being implemented because this leader mounted a concerted effort to sell the problem and has built a powerful guiding coalition.

4. AGITATING WITH A BROKEN HEART

A fourth element that characterizes kingdom leaders who effectively agitate for kingdom engagement is the heart. In this case, I mean a broken heart. Kingdom leaders work for change with a passion born of pain.

Kingdom leaders can choose from plenty of barriers that stand in the way of people experiencing the life God intends for them. Substantial issues lie in every arena of human ex-istence—from education to mental health to physical fitness to emotional stability to financial security to spiritual devel-opment. It's my observation that some aspects of these human ills break leaders' hearts. It may grab them because it has deeply impacted them or someone close to them in a negative way. The situation has gotten under their skin and has captured not just their imagination but also their emo-tional commitment. They can't *not* agitate for something to be done about it.

This broken heart fuels both leaders' passion and their pa-tience. Unless leaders are gripped emotionally by a situation, they may not have the energy and persuasiveness to sell the problem or expend the effort to build a coalition. These heart-broken leaders agitate to move people's hearts for a cause they've staked their own heart on, and they're driven not to give up easily or quickly. They work from the conviction that, however long it takes, they will pursue their mission.

People sense this level of commitment in a leader. This explains why people join or adopt the leader's cause or sign up for the leader's team. Mere angry agitation turns people off over time, driving them away. (I've seen it happen.) But an agitating leader motivated by compassion proves attractive.

When Carl and Mary talk about the plight of foster children and what can be done to help this special group in our population, they know what they're talking about. They've had more than thirty foster children live with them through the years, all the way from babies to teenagers. And they've adopted some of them. They cry when they talk about them.

For several decades, they've served as president of their state's foster parents association. Operating from a broken heart, they've sold the problem by helping to educate people about the needs of these children. They have the political savvy to move the ball down the field for this cause, working with multiple state agencies and the legislature.

They've been dissatisfied the whole time—and they've made sure some important people knew it. The coalition they cobbled together works in multiple venues—from schools to social services—to improve the help foster children receive. Carl and Mary are master agitators—kingdom leaders championing the chance for thousands of kids to experience more of the life God intends for them.

5. AGITATING WITH THE END IN MIND

Kingdom collaborators keep their eyes on the finish line. As Paul eloquently said in Philippians 3:14, they "press on toward the goal to win the prize" they have been called to pursue. Several perspectives help them not to lose sight of their vision.

First, they know that it's not about them. Though they may become branded as the spokesperson or the "face" for a project or effort, they know the cause they champion is bigger than they are. This awareness must rise to the level of conviction to fend off temptations to give in to the current celebrity craze. Effective kingdom leaders don't allow themselves to become the subject of the narrative; they point people to the issue or societal ill they care about.

Closely related to this first awareness is the second: these leaders expect conflict. They don't overpersonalize the resistance they encounter, which would only make it all about them again. Instead, they realize that people can't get from Egypt to the Promised Land without going through the wilderness. In the Exodus saga, the wilderness sojourn was in a dangerous territory where people pushed back against the leader and selected whether or not to experience God's preferred future. Modern-day wildernesses have the same dynamics. Leading people through this space always sets the leader up for criticism. Some people question the direction and actions of the leader, others blame the leader for anything that goes wrong, while still others lobby for a return to the familiar, even with its problems.

Third, kingdom leaders who agitate effectively don't merely practice deconstruction. They offer hope that situations and circumstances can be improved, that problems can be addressed and even solved. These leaders understand that merely rehearsing a problem proves debilitating over time. People need some hope that if they join the leader, they will have a chance to succeed in making a better world.

We could learn something from the perspective of the discussions underway in South Africa's post-apartheid era. South Africans don't ignore the past; they commemorate it. (I toured the Apartheid Museum in Soweto and the prison on Robben Island, where the struggle for freedom and equality is commemorated.) But they don't let the past define the conversation. Their narrative is about moving forward. Despite challenges (unemployment, crime and corruption, ongoing prejudice), many South Africans see themselves as part of the solution as they forge a better future for their country.

These leaders take their cue from Mandela's own story. Through the many years of his imprisonment, he never stopped agitating. His letters and writings were smuggled out to the outside world (with the help of a prison guard). He never took his eye off the ball. The end in mind kept Mandela going. And those he helped liberate are following his example.

Want to be a great kingdom collaborator? Figure out what breaks your heart. Get really good at selling the problem. Gather people around you who have the connections and wisdom to leverage your heartache into kingdom advancement.

What are you waiting for? You've got some agitating to do!

Next time you're in Fort Worth, Texas, check out the restaurant called Brewed. It's a great watering hole, place to eat, and social hotspot. It's also a church.

Brewed is the brainchild and work of Joey Turner and others who understand that most people aren't shopping for a worship service to attend but are on the hunt for a great place to eat and to socialize. Joey and company approach church planting through community development—creating a kingdom expression of church. They planted Brewed on the corner of a drug-infested street lined with shuttered buildings. That was then. Now, several years later, the success of the restaurant has helped to spark a renaissance in the area. Art galleries and specialty stores have moved in and operate in a revitalized and robust business and social community. Brewed pioneered the way. Its story shows what happens when the kingdom breaks into enemy territory.

Journey across the metroplex to downtown Dallas. Actually, a little north and east of downtown lies an area known as Deep Ellum. For years, the area languished as drugs and crime ate away at its social and commercial fabric. The situation became so desperate that one local politician opined, "There is no life in Deep Ellum." The statement captured the thinking of most people familiar with the area. But for Joel and Rachel, that pronouncement sounded like an opportunity for God to show up and show off. So they started Life in Deep Ellum, a kingdom outpost, to begin the restoration of a part of the city others had given up on.

Life in Deep Ellum has a physical presence as a coffee shop, an art gallery, a music venue (in its heyday, the area boasted lots of music venues), and a shared workspace—all of which help to pay for the building. There's also a recovery ministry—and, oh yeah, a worship service on Sundays attracting several hundred people who are journeying toward God.

The architect who gave me the tour of the place (himself a Jesus-follower) picked the locale for his office expressly because it generates spiritual conversations with clients who visit and because the "vibe" expresses authentic community to him.

I like food and coffee as much as anybody, but that's not the point of these stories. The point is that a growing number of kingdom expressions demonstrate a combination of social and spiritual entrepreneurship on the part of the leaders who dream up and power these operations. By describing these leaders' entrepreneurship as "social and spiritual," I don't mean that they have two different kinds of entrepreneurship. Their entrepreneurial efforts impact both the social *and* the spiritual arenas.

What characterizes these leaders? How are they different? What mindsets and competencies do they possess that distinguish them as kingdom entrepreneurs? These questions form the subject of this chapter's investigation.

THEY SEE OPPORTUNITIES WHERE OTHERS SEE PROBLEMS

Those who focus on obstacles figure out why things can't happen. Entrepreneurs spend their energy on looking for solutions. They see problems as possibilities that just haven't been adequately explored and addressed.

Kingdom collaborators use entrepreneurial energy and thinking to tackle big societal issues. Generational poverty, human trafficking, illiteracy, alcohol and drug addiction—these are mammoth problems that plague our culture. Add to this list the devastation and despair that ransacks the human spirit of those involved, and you have a potent recipe for a sense of helplessness and a reason to be overwhelmed by the scale of the pain and suffering. In the face of these daunting challenges, kingdom leaders not only choose *not* to sound the retreat; they charge ahead! They aren't reckless. They just believe that God has called them to something important that they must do. These leaders are determined to be part of a solution.

Some years ago, Larry James took over a food pantry and clothes closet that was on shaky ground. Today CitySquare in Dallas has a multimillion-dollar annual budget addressing issues from food challenges to employment training to immigration to the seemingly intractable challenge of homelessness. I remember Larry's comment to a group of leaders I had taken to see his operation: "We've discovered that the cure for homelessness is to give people a home!" That conviction has enabled Larry and his team to provide hundreds of formerly homeless people a home.

Most organizations and communities approach the problem of homelessness with a "provide food and shelter" solution, warehousing the homeless population in overnight quarters and providing them meals. This is a focus-on-the-problem approach. For Larry and his ministry staff, that simply isn't good enough. They see the situation as providing an opportunity to furnish people a home. This conviction, combined with some innovative thinking and funding, has resulted in transitioning people from living on the streets to having a place to call home.

THEY DEVELOP A HIGH CAPACITY FOR RISK AND A TOLERANCE FOR FAILURE

I met the church leadership team on Skype. They wanted to talk with me about a $25-million opportunity they were considering. The money wasn't even a big part of the conversation. Our discussion focused on how the congregation's purchase of a ten-acre campus and facilities in their town would position them to expand their ministry as well as change the culture of their church.

I was impressed with how they had done their homework. I was even more impressed with their confidence: they were relaxed in their deliberations on great opportunity while also regarding a situation fraught with risk and potential failure. In short, I knew I was dealing with leaders who had a large capacity for risk and tolerance of failure.

Entrepreneurs risk. But they don't do so rashly. The effective ones do their homework. They gather intelligence. They investigate the options. They weigh the downside risk against the upside potential. This distinguishes them from the herd. Most assess only the potential downsides, but these leaders first explore the possibilities they envision and only then weigh their options. They may be willing to bet the farm, but only if the potential return seems promising and probable to them. Unlike leaders who are overly cautious—whose next decision will be their first—entrepreneurial leaders understand that they may not (probably don't) have perfect information and that some significant unknowns may (and probably do) exist despite their best attempt to anticipate negative results from their actions or initiative.

Sometimes these entrepreneurial leaders get it wrong. They fail—on occasion, hugely. For many spiritual leaders, it seems that failure is not an option. They have no theology to support it, notwithstanding a boatload of biblical literature bearing witness to leaders' failures, both personal and public. Nor do they have the psychological resilience to deal with it. Unlike kingdom entrepreneurs—who expect to make some wrong calls—they suffer from the need to be right, the need not to make mistakes. This attitude blinds them to the opportunity that comes cloaked as a problem. Whereas the entrepreneur sees failure as a necessary part of a continuum of learning, the average leader sees failure as the final word.

The entrepreneurial leader also never views failure as a possibility that must be avoided. As one leader wrote to me this week: "We don't always know what we're doing, but we've got the guts to try and aren't afraid of failure!" That's the spirit of entrepreneurial kingdom leaders. They possess the capacity to get up off the mat after a failure and get back into the game. They aren't finished; rather, they just made a mistake they've learned from, an error in judgment they won't make again.

A leader for whom I have high regard is well known for his serial innovations in his field. Several years ago, in an expansion of his enterprise, he made a mistake. He saw—correctly—an opportunity to expand his market penetration into a new demographic in his city's population. But he put the wrong leadership team in place to run the initiative. After eighteen frustrating and costly months, he shut down the project.

He could have chosen to play the blame game by disgracing the failed team, making an object lesson of them. What would that have accomplished, except to instill in the rest of his organization the lesson that failure wouldn't be tolerated? Instead, this wise leader honored the efforts of the team. Though unsuccessful, they had worked hard and exhibited good character. They had discovered what wouldn't work.

And the leader held a luncheon in their honor. The failure wasn't swept under the rug. There was no lack of transparency. Disappointment was expressed. But hard-working people weren't thrown under the bus for trying, so their work could still be celebrated.

What do you think this leader's approach builds into an organization? The answer is loyalty, camaraderie, high esprit de corps, the confidence to keep trying till they got a win. Is this the kind of organizational culture you want to have? Such a culture comes only when risk and failure are not only tolerated but also appreciated.

Think back to Jesus' dealings with his disciples. He took an incredible risk when he handed over the kingdom movement to those few early followers. And they blew it often. James and John asked Jesus if they could call down fire from heaven on a Samaritan village that didn't welcome them; at the Mount of Transfiguration, they couldn't cast out a demon; when the whole operation seemed to be collapsing, they ran and hid; and those who stayed denied their relationship with Jesus. Really? This was the crew Jesus had in mind for leading a movement to charge the gates of hell?

What was he thinking? It's simple. He saw the upside potential of a world made better. He took the chance that people would experience the life God intends for them. In short, the vision of the kingdom of God proved too powerful a possibility not to put his disciples into play, knowing that some failures would ensue.

THEY PRACTICE ABUNDANCE— NOT SCARCITY—THINKING

I don't know her name. All I know is that she wanted to talk. We were seated beside each other on a plane. I was heading home from speaking to a large gathering earlier in the day in a downtown convention center. Some of the conventioneers who had heard me speak were on that flight. As they passed me on the way to their seats, they acknowledged me and said kind things about my presentation.

"You have a lot of friends," my seatmate observed. When I explained what was going on, she asked me the topic of my presentations. I told her the gist of it: churches adopting a people-development agenda by helping people grow into their own skin through serving others. Then I drifted off into a short nap.

When I woke up (I didn't want to miss the snack basket), she was waiting and eager to tell her story. "I think I'm not sitting here by accident," she began. She cried as she shared her dream of being able to help homeless people not just to have shelter but to acquire a home, have jobs, and be restored to a better life. "People have told me I can't do it, that it's too big a problem for me to tackle." I encouraged her to follow her broken heart, and I gave her names and places where some adaptive solutions to big problems are being implemented. Most of all, I told her not to pay attention to those whose world is too small for her passion.

Scarcity thinking abounds. The woman on the plane had been served a steady diet of it. It seductively postures itself as insightful, realistic, and astute. Common phrases like "there is not enough of this" or "we don't have what it takes" come across as informed awareness and a reasoned point of view. The frequent conclusion is that situations can't be changed and positive progress can't be made (or even attempted).

There's no way to calculate the number of dreams like my seat-mate's that have been quashed by such thinking and the number of people whose lives have been robbed of betterment because a scarcity mentality postponed or derailed action.

Kingdom leaders, on the other hand, practice abundance thinking. When others see a lunch basket as inadequate to feed a crowd of thousands, kingdom leaders begin working with what they have, believing that God can multiply resources and efforts to accomplish something truly remarkable. This is the phenomenon Jesus referenced when he said that faith even the size of a tiny mustard seed would release the power of God into situations. His life and ministry proved his point. With the whole world to save, he poured himself into a few followers whom he infected with a kingdom vision so strong that it still inspires over twenty centuries later.

Entrepreneurial leaders don't limit their thinking to questions like "how much will it cost?" or "where will we find this money in our budget?" They think in terms of "how much will it cost us if we *don't* do this?" Their analysis, while it doesn't ignore costs, includes the loss of opportunity. These leaders think of the upside potential of taking certain actions, of investing resources into ideas.

Dan wrote to me today of his plan to "circle the schools" in his Northern California city. He's a business guy who understands the link between literacy and life, both for individuals and for the community. His plan involves starting a literacy initiative in a couple of elementary schools where he has relational connections and involving a couple of congregations with leaders who have a heart for helping kids read and succeed. Then he'll expand to include businesses and other community organizations in the effort. Dan sees the cuts in the state education budget as an opportunity for more community engagement in the classroom. This thinking reflects an entrepreneurial mentality.

Entrepreneurial kingdom leaders face forward. Many people—and sadly, many leaders—face the other direction. Tied to the past, they make predictions and plans based on yesterday's results. Maxims like "the best prediction of future behavior is past performance" and "there's nothing new under the sun" characterize their thinking. A rear-view perspective certainly captures some truth in its sights, but it's an incomplete way of seeing. It reflects the reality of scarcity thinking, limited to building the future on the shoulders of the past.

Kingdom leaders lash themselves to the future. They believe that the kingdom represents God's preferred future for people, communities, and the world. This conviction shapes both their attitudes and their actions. These leaders don't believe that the future is completely beholden to the past. They look for inflection points for charting a new course, starting a new conversation, setting a new trajectory. Their abundance thinking permits them the enthusiasm and vision powered by the perspective that the best is yet to come.

Treating these leaders as Pollyannas is a huge mistake, as if they aren't acquainted with the challenges of today's world. On the contrary, these kingdom leaders engage their communities and the needs around them and are in touch personally with the current pain and suffering that people bear. Rather than letting present-day realities trim their expectations, those realities stoke the fires of these leaders' ambitions for a better world. They point to the harsh realities as evidence that God has something better in mind.

While writing this chapter, I had lunch with Bishop Milton Grannum of New Covenant Church in Philadelphia. He is seventy-five years old and going strong, proactively setting the stage for the next phase of the congregation he has pastored for over four decades. When he arrived in the United States in 1967 from the Caribbean, he had twenty-seven cents in his pocket. He also had God. Today the New Covenant campus sprawls over forty acres, with more than a dozen historical buildings on the campus of an old college that the congregation purchased some years ago.

Bishop Grannum and his team are strategizing on how to leverage these facilities into a community development center. Building a great congregation has captured him for forty years; building a great community has become his passion. Most folks his age are thinking about cutting back. The bishop is thinking about multiplying. This is abundant thinking— kingdom thinking in pursuit of kingdom dreams.

To face forward in our country today means to stare into a culture that's far less open to church-as-institution than in previous decades. The increasing disaffection with organized religion has been well documented. And this trend is not a fad. It represents a sea change. Answers for navigating these waters aren't found in history books. Only those leaders open to something new have a chance of figuring out how we can partner with the mission of God in the decades ahead.

The good news is that church-as-movement—in other words, church that demonstrates a kingdom-centric agenda—offers a way forward. Even better news is that God is not caught off guard with this development. He isn't struggling to figure out how he's going to pursue his mission. His kingdom—life as he intends—has never been more relevant or urgent. Entrepreneurial spiritual leaders don't fear the future; they welcome it!

THEY KNOW HOW TO BUILD MOMENTUM

In their wonderful volume on leading organizational change (*Effective Change Leadership*, Crisp Publications, 1991), Cynthia Scott and Dennis Jaffe share strategies for leaders who are managing change and transition. They identified four stages, or quadrants, that describe organizational dynamics when change is underway: denial, resistance, exploration, and commitment. Entrepreneurial leaders call out organizational denial, which typically leads to resistance. The outcome of the struggle in this phase determines whether the organization retreats into denial or pushes forward into exploration. The exploration phase marks the turn of the organization from a past orientation to a future orientation.

Having pushed through resistance, the leader and organization now have permission to risk new initiatives, to try new approaches and pursue fresh ideas. Over time, the gains made in these efforts coalesce into an organizational commitment to long-term systemic change.

One of the strategies for navigating the exploration phase of transition is creating and building momentum to support the change that's underway. Effective leaders do this by identifying some short-term, surefire wins they can pull off quickly and relatively easily. These wins demonstrate the positive results of the new approach and also highlight the ability of the organization to meet the challenges of the new chapter. Entrepreneurial leaders understand that a basic requirement for a leader is to help people not only to dream, but also to believe that they can accomplish their dreams and live into their aspirations.

Yesterday my email contained an update from a business leader who wants to build a literacy coalition in his city. The strategy he outlined in his correspondence involved working with a couple of congregations that are willing to partner in serving some poorly performing schools in the district. In his words, "If we can get a couple of winning stories out of their experiences, I feel we can begin to attract other business groups, social organizations, and congregations to come on board in this effort." His is a smart approach because it involves establishing momentum that will attract resources into a new and important community endeavor. This is the kind of thinking and leadership that entrepreneurial kingdom leaders practice.

THEY USE ADAPTIVE APPROACHES
TO PROBLEM SOLVING

Entrepreneurial kingdom leaders engage their challenges with an adaptive leadership approach. The term "adaptive leadership" was coined by Harvard leadership professors Ronald Heifetz and Marty Linsky in their insightful book *Leadership on the Line* (Harvard Business School, 2002). They contrast that phrase with what they call "technical solutions." Technical problem solving works when problems can be easily identified and addressed with quick, cut-and-dried approaches that require little or only targeted changes that aren't disruptive to the organization.

Rather than tweaking old approaches (technical solutions), adaptive leadership boldly attacks problems with new solutions. Adaptive change addresses problems that aren't easily identified or understood. The presenting issues of a problem don't always reveal the underlying causes. Adaptive leaders insist on facing the brutal facts, challenging unproductive norms, and asking penetrating and sometimes uncomfortable questions in their quest to understand the problem.

Adaptive solutioning often involves experimenting, which typically causes organizational disruption. New approaches, new roles, and new relationships may be called for across a wide spectrum of organizational life and activity. Adaptive leaders work to involve the people impacted by a problem in finding and implementing solutions.

Michael Sorrell serves as a great example of this adaptive leadership approach. He is president of Paul Quinn College, a historic black college on the south side of Dallas. When

Sorrell assumed his role in 2007, he took on a college facing a financial challenge and a dismal graduation rate of only 1 percent. He understood right away that mere tweaks to existing approaches weren't going to turn the school around. The situation called for new vision, which in turn required radically new action and some drastic approaches to support it. These new approaches had widespread ramifications for the various constituencies involved: students, faculty, parents, donors, and the community.

President Sorrell decided that the college could no longer afford a football program (they were losing money and games). But what he did next demonstrates adaptive entrepreneurial thinking. Shutting down a cost center (the football program) is a technical solution. Turning the old football field into an urban farm where students are required to work (and awarded with tuition credits) was an adaptive solution.

Other implemented ideas addressed the culture of the school and the students. Requiring students to attend classes in business attire challenged their mindset and prepared them for the professional workplace. Forging internship programs with local businesses provided companies with good help as a return for investing money in the school. For the students, it meant having a better chance at securing a job upon graduation. The result of this overhaul of the school is not ony improved graduation rates but, more importantly, a culture shift that challenged and addressed underlying issues that had perpetuated poor performance.

Perhaps Sorrell's background allowed him to be adaptive. He didn't come to the school presidency from an academic or educational domain. He was an attorney and White House adviser. So his field of vision for solutions wasn't constricted to traditional options. By not being steeped (and trapped) in typical approaches, Sorrell could "move to the balcony," a phrase Heifetz and Linsky use to describe a leadership strategy that provides the leader with emotional distance and greater perspective on situations they face. This allowed him to see a larger playing field than a football gridiron. "There is more than one field of dreams," Sorrell told a PBS reporter who interviewed him as part of a documentary detailing his novel approaches to college education.

We would be wrong to conclude that leaders *can't* grow beyond the leadership thinking and approaches typical of their domain. Just moments ago, I received an email from Tony, a pastor in northwest Alabama, who has proven his leadership capabilities as a pastor by developing a thriving congregation with improvements in all the church-centric measures. But he has been willing to move his leadership parameters from pastoring a congregation to seeing himself as a community developer.

Tony's set of concerns and competencies has expanded significantly. He informed me, "We are now the owner/ operator of a small diner on the square. Our goal is to offer short-term employment to train servers and short-order cooks. . . . Applicants will be those that genuinely want to break out of a cycle of generational poverty." After updating me on the congregation's adoption of a local elementary school, he reported, "The principal is giving us access to parents that also want to break out of generational poverty.

We will teach them life skills." Tony's congregation and community are never going to be the same.

The kind of issues that engage kingdom leaders—huge societal challenges involving poverty, illiteracy, and human trafficking, to name a few obvious ones—require adaptive solutions. Entrepreneurial leaders not steeped and trapped in church-as-institution approaches will lead the kingdom endeavors that tackle these life-diminishing dilemmas.

Kingdom collaborators combine social and spiritual entrepreneurship. They express confidence that proves contagious. Their approach helps others see opportunity instead of problems. They aren't afraid to take risks, knowing that failure is certain only if they don't try. These leaders have an abundance mentality that frees up the King's resources. By facing forward, they paint a vision of a preferred future that captures people's imaginations. They start with what they have rather than merely lamenting what they don't have. Their strategies create momentum that attracts others into their endeavors. Their adaptive approaches craft new solutions that yield positive and often unexpected results.

These entrepreneurial kingdom collaborators serve as sluice gates for the kingdom of God to pour into their communities, improving the lives of people around them. Their communities and neighborhoods are reclaimed from the dark kingdom that has stolen away the life God intends. The kingdom comes!

MARRY VISION AND ACTION

ABOUT THIRTY OF US crowded into the room to hear John Sibert, the president and chief operating officer of CitySquare in Dallas (mentioned in the previous chapter). We had just finished taking a tour of their two-year-old main campus, which includes their massive food operations and employment training center as well as their educational facilities. We were also able to inspect one of their fifty new cabins about to be opened as a housing village.

Appropriately impressed with the scope of the $15-million annual operation, our group was eager to hear from one of the organization's key leaders of this kingdom enterprise in one of our country's major cities. John took questions, responding candidly about their struggles as well as their obvious successes. Despite the appearance of the organization being well-organized and highly functional, John admitted to the chaos that accompanies the kind of work they do—the balancing act of working with multiple constituencies, the ever-changing landscape of governmental regulations, along with the constant need for raising money to support an organization that employs over 130 people full-time while providing services to thousands of people every month. John quipped, "If you can't handle a chaotic environment, you probably won't do well here."

John further observed, "Not everything we try works." One of their organizational mantras is "fail fast." He explained the philosophy undergirding this approach by saying, "We have a bias toward action." Rather than seeing itself as a think tank for discussion of strategies and policies, CitySquare throws itself into applying multiple approaches to provide solutions to problems, learning as they go, adapting by doing.

Kingdom collaborators aren't pied pipers who prey on people's need to follow. Nor are they troubadours who entertain listeners with pleasing melodies. They marry vision with action. Kingdom leaders inspire people's imaginations to possibilities, but they also energize people to action. They convince people to work toward a better world, to achieve epic wins that roll back the debilitating forces of the anti-life kingdom that ravage human existence. Kingdom leaders aren't content to raise a crowd of spectators; they want to launch an invasion force. Like the star of the good Samaritan parable, people influenced by kingdom leaders get off their donkeys to deliver real help in situations of need.

In short, kingdom collaborators marry vision with action.

THEY INCARNATE VISION-VALUE ALIGNMENT

Kingdom leaders operate from a strong vision for a preferred future. They don't ignore the past, but they act to change the future. The course of action they adopt reflects their personal and particular values. These values often provide the motivation behind their vision (for example, justice, mercy, compassion, respect, responsibility, freedom, integrity, healthy relationships). Vision and values align in the very lives of effective kingdom leaders.

Savvy leaders know that values are more often caught than taught. They understand that what people do is what they believe; any other claims of belief is just talk. This means values are behaviorally examined and communicated. It further means that a leader's followers determine and evaluate what she believes, based on her observable actions. To maintain integrity and credibility, the leader's own actions must be consistent with her stated values.

Consider Jesus' leadership at this point. He demonstrated a one-to-one correspondence between his teaching and his action. Everything he did gave meaning to his admonition for his disciples to "seek first the kingdom of God" (Matthew 6:33). His praying, his healing, his touch, his availability, his compassion, his commitment to the poor—all incarnated his kingdom vision and values. His instruction to "love your enemies and pray for those who persecute you," along with his challenge to his disciples to turn the other cheek when mistreated (Matthew 5:39, 44), gain traction as rules for living because of Jesus' own behavior, especially during his last hours and days on earth.

The vital connection between vision and action informs one of the most frequent challenges I issue to leaders who want to be change agents: "Go first" is the shorthand version. "Do whatever it is you want to see done" is the more complete idea. And then there's Gandhi's famous dictum: "Be the change you want to see." Church-centric people often need a real-life example to help them see what it means to adopt a more kingdom-centric agenda—to see themselves as viral kingdom agents. Kingdom leaders set the example by and through their lives.

Mt. Pleasant, Texas, has the good fortune to have such a kingdom leader as its superintendent of education. Titus County Cares, a faith-based community service organization in the town, developed a literacy initiative involving volunteer readers who read weekly with at-risk kids in the local elementary schools. When the call went out to the community for volunteer readers, the superintendent was one of the first to sign up. Imagine that! A superintendent of education volunteering to read one hour a week to an at-risk second-grade boy in his own district!

SAVVY LEADERS KNOW THAT VALUES ARE MORE OFTEN CAUGHT THAN TAUGHT.

No wonder, then, that the principals of the local schools in the district followed his lead by volunteering also. The middle school principal has encouraged her teachers to use their lunch hour or preparation period to journey off-campus to read to elementary school students. And townspeople have taken notice; now 150 volunteers in this large town read every week in every elementary school. Retired teachers join firefighters, sheriff's deputies, stay-at-home moms, attorneys, and healthcare providers to give kids a better shot at life by teaching them to read. The vision of a community rallying around a literacy initiative has become a reality because people saw leaders showing the way.

Movements aren't conceived and led from the commentator's booth. They live or die on the field of play. The ones that make it have leaders whose values (behavior) align with the vision of the movement. Jesus showed us the kingdom by how he lived and what he did. Today's kingdom leaders do the same.

THEY BUILD ON-RAMPS FOR OTHERS TO JOIN THE ACTION

Kingdom leaders always strategize on how to make it possible for others to get in on the action. They build multiple on-ramps to create access for others to join the movement.

When I urge leaders to "go first" in leading a movement, I also include an important corollary: "don't go alone." With this advice, I'm advocating an on-ramp with various lanes. One goal simply involves exposing people to the kingdom virus by introducing them to a kingdom initiative. Some who are exposed will catch the virus and become viral agents themselves, acting to infect others. The apprentice on-ramp involves hands-on direction by the leaders. Sometimes the apprentice is expected to take over the work of the leader. In other cases, the apprentice is expected to develop other apprentices to multiply the workforce.

One leader of a congregation I know regularly scans the crowd of worshippers to identify potential leaders for various community projects. As he sees faces, he remembers conversations and interactions he has had with parishioners in which they've expressed interest in a particular issue or ministry. Because of his intentional reflection, when a new serving opportunity opens (either in the congregation or in the community), he already has a leader or group of volunteers in mind who can shoulder the work. Connecting people with their passions ensures that a highly motivated workforce will tackle the assignment.

This past weekend, I visited Hillspring Church in Richland, Washington, a congregation I've been working with over the past six years. The pastor, Bryan White, assumed leadership when the founding pastor of the church retired after serving for more than two decades. Those familiar with this kind of pastoral succession know that it contains dynamics that can create a very precarious situation. A successful leadership transition requires sterling character and high emotional intelligence on the part of the new pastor, in addition to the obvious competencies required for pastoral leadership. Often the new pastor becomes a casualty in the process because the transition dynamics go awry or are poorly managed. (Refer to the previous chapter's discussion of the transition of organizations and leaders.) Bryan has successfully navigated these treacherous rapids and is firmly ensconced as the leader.

Bryan and his team are intentionally and increasingly fashioning a kingdom ministry agenda. One of the strategies paying huge dividends has been launching people into ministry areas that congregation members identify as a need and as something they have a heart for. Two new community engagement initiatives were instigated and led by members of the congregation. These efforts were not the brainchild of the staff or elders, but emerged out of two members' hearts and minds.

One new ministry targets women who have had miscarriages, a painful and common experience. Most people are left to deal with such losses on their own, so the new group will provide a community of care that will connect people who have had miscarriages in the past with those who have recently experienced one. The other new ministry will connect with women who suddenly find themselves alone and single, either through divorce or the death of their spouse. This life situation involves not only grieving but often a significant repositioning of relationships with friends, who may seem difficult to connect with socially and emotionally.

Hillspring's vision statement contains two prominent and powerful words: *hope* and *compassion*. Both express the heartbeat of this community of Jesus-followers. Those who engage the community are celebrated along with those who provide the church's usual ministry and organizational functions. The leaders have crafted this environment by developing a coaching culture that helps people identify and develop their passions, which often involves significant engagement with community needs. The leaders use "kingdom speak" in their gatherings, telling stories, celebrating life transformation, honoring community leaders. These efforts make it easy for people to move from calling to commitment. In other words, they have successfully created on-ramps for people to move into kingdom engagement.

Unfortunately I know far too many church environments that erect roadblocks rather than build on-ramps. These can take many shapes. There may be excessive command-and-control elements when it comes to ministry authorization and engagement. Too much insistence on church-centric ministry can also limit community engagement. Communication roadblocks create barriers to ministry incubation by restricting information that would allow people access to areas of need. Or an organization or ministry culture may fail in helping people who have a specific passion develop the skills they need to be effective in pursuing their ministry interests.

Kingdom leaders actively pursue strategies that develop and deploy viral kingdom agents—people who help people live the life God intends for them. On the other hand, leaders who operate within a Lone Ranger paradigm, who see themselves as the primary ministry-giver, restrict the flow of kingdom life by failing to create ways for people to get involved in helping others.

THEY GET THE RIGHT PEOPLE TO THE TABLE

Strategic and effective kingdom leaders marry vision and action by making sure they get the right people involved in addressing a problem or pursuing an initiative. This concern ranges from assembling the appropriate team to coming up with solutions to making sure the people who are affected by proposed courses of action can participate in the decision making. The price of not paying attention to this important aspect shows up in stymied efforts, or worse. The effect can prove deadly to an initiative, especially if the people who are essential to project implementation are left out of the planning. A project can be intentionally sabotaged by an individual or group left out of the planning process, especially if they're stakeholders in the issue being addressed or if the proposed solution impinges on the efforts already underway.

I can illustrate this dynamic from my own consulting experience. For eighteen months, I worked with a group on a literacy effort for their community. The initial strategy involved finding and cultivating leaders in the faith sector to become involved, then moving on to engage leaders in other domains (education, business, healthcare, government, etc.). The educational community proved supportive, so we tried to establish a new campaign, initially expressed as a summer reading program but designed to move into classroom reading and after-school engagements. Strategy meetings went well, but conversations away from the table went nowhere. The group couldn't gain any traction to turn ideas into implementation. I became increasingly puzzled when my visits with the group every four months or so uncovered very little progress, despite the group's enthusiasm and commitment to the project.

Then someone on the strategy-planning group had the insight that unlocked all the doors to community buy-in and engagement. This member raised the question whether the effort to create a new literacy initiative had unwittingly created apprehension among groups who were already working in this space. "Perhaps they're seeing us as a threat," he said, "a competitive group that's going to be vying with them for volunteers and other resources." He went on, "If they're feeling this way and expressing this suspicion to their constituencies, it could explain why we keep running into brick walls."

This hunch proved to be spot-on. The group discovered that its proposed new campaign was meeting with active resistance from more than a dozen existing groups.

The next move by the crew I was working with turned a potential dead-on-arrival initiative into an energized cross-domain community effort. The group decided that rather than create a new "it" to attack illiteracy, they would create a literacy coalition, one designed to lift all ships with the rising tide. Now, rather than being seen as a threatening competitor by existing groups, the new literacy coalition represented a new ally in the battle against a crippling societal ill. While celebrating current efforts, the new effort doesn't preclude new projects being launched. In fact, this collaborative approach has opened possibilities that new initiatives will have the full support of existing organizations.

The decision to develop a literacy coalition brought the right people to the table. When the coalition was formerly launched, the event included representatives from the education sector (school board members), the business community (sponsors who had signed on), the faith community (some of the original visionaries along with new recruits), and most importantly, leaders of the existing literacy programs. The original plan was replaced, and the size and makeup of the group ensured follow-up action.

An often-overlooked dynamic when addressing problems is getting people who are directly affected by problems to be part of the solution process. Planners grow frustrated by the failure of people they're working *for* to adopt proposed solutions or put energy or enthusiasm into implementation efforts. A simple but powerful shift in prepositions goes a long way toward eliminating this frustration. Rather than working *for* people, it's better to work *with* people when they're affected by the problem or by any solution addressing the issue. People need to get their own skin in the game.

President Sorrell at Paul Quinn College proves this point (in the previous chapter, he was our example of adaptive leadership). By getting businesses to invest in hiring interns, he brought them to the table as partners. By growing food for a population living in a food desert, he promoted engagement by his students. By allowing students to work for their tuition, he created an enthusiastic and engaged student body rather than encouraging a culture where recipients had none of their skin in the game other than showing up for class. By bringing the various constituents together, Sorrell put people around the table to figure out a new model of the urban college. They all stand to be impacted by whatever approach they determine to take. As Sorrell said in a PBS interview about his work, "Someone will figure out the urban college solution. It might as well be the people who are involved in it."

Getting the right eyes on the problem and the right people at the table raises the chance not only that a preferred future (vision) will be implemented (action) but also that adaptive approaches will accelerate and improve solutions.

THEY MANAGE VOLUNTEERS WELL

Many kingdom expressions—especially those engaging community issues—require the involvement of volunteers either on a project basis or as an ongoing effort.

Too many social agencies, not-for-profit organizations, and churches misuse, mistreat, or underserve their volunteers. I'm not suggesting that they do this intentionally. Usually it's the result of one or more frequent failures: (1) failure to see things from the volunteer's perspective, (2) failure to connect the volunteers' actions to the vision of the effort, and (3) failure to honor the efforts of volunteers appropriately.

1. Failure to see things from the volunteer's perspective. I jumped in the van with the rest of my church group, ready to go to work for the evening. We had volunteered to work in a feeding program for the homeless in our city. We arrived early, jazzed about the opportunity to share Jesus' love in a tangible way with people who need it. Then our orientation by the permanent staff began. After we were each given our assignment for the meal service (mine was to dip baked beans from cooking pots onto plates as part of the food-line assembly process), we received instructions about our engagement with the homeless people themselves. No talking to people as we served them; the conversation would slow down the line. And no sitting with the homeless during the mealtime. The fellowship would slow down the meal, pushing the cleanup later than desired into the evening.

The closest I got to a homeless person during the evening was four meal assemblers away from the serving window, camped out at my station at the stove. (When I wasn't quick enough, I was "encouraged" by the staff to pick up the pace.) The scorecard for the feeding organization became crystal clear: get the food distributed and meal finished as fast as possible. Neither my group nor I have been back to serve dinner.

Probably at some point the feeding ministry cared for the homeless population and the hunger challenge they face. However, as time went on and practices developed, efficiency in food distribution trumped personal engagement between those serving and those served. This nightly feeding was provided *for* the recipients, not intended to be a meal *with* them.

Volunteers like our group were put off by agenda. I didn't set aside an evening to journey downtown to sling beans on a plate. Our group's motivation came from compassion for the homeless. We anticipated that we would have personal interactions with real people. However, the process of food distribution centering on efficiency squelched our motivation. In fact, we felt misused, since the recruitment of our team had pitched to our heart and compassion.

I'm sure the organization scores high in serving meals in record time; that's just not the goal shared by volunteers who answer the call to share love and care through a meal. The food ministry leadership needs to think through the experience from the volunteer's perspective. I'm confident that reordering their approach based on this reflection would help them not have to spend as much energy recruiting fresh volunteers.

2. Failure to connect the volunteers' actions to the vision of the effort. My experience with the food ministry also illustrates the second frequent failure organizations make when dealing with volunteers: disconnecting or not providing connection between vision and action. When volunteers perceive that their efforts are aligned with the vision and values of the organization, their role is elevated as is the importance of the work they do. The heightening of role and mission motivate volunteers in multiple ways, from boosting performance to increasing their reliability and accountability for their work.

One organization I resource is a well-respected national faith-based ministry. In my home city, they engage an army of volunteers during the Christmas season to collect and distribute toys, games, and bicycles to hundreds of families who have limited economic resources. For several years, I've encouraged this organization not just to direct volunteers to their assignment, but also to spend a moment or two with groups and individuals connecting their efforts to the organization's ultimate motive of sharing God's love with the economically challenged people of our community.

Many of the volunteers have no faith background themselves and don't automatically associate their efforts with the celebration of God's good will to come to earth in the birth of his Son. A brief conversation would make this connection. Offering to pray with volunteers for their own needs would also go a long way toward accomplishing this connection and increasing the possibility of additional spiritual dialogue or exploration on the volunteer's part.

The argument I sometimes encounter is that we shouldn't push our faith on others. That's not what I'm talking about. I'm talking about coming out of the closet and admitting that we are Jesus-followers and are motivated by his love for people and by his direction that we do the same as his disciples. Besides, I've met very few people who are offended when prayer is offered on their behalf. People who serve also need to be served. Their needs may be different from those who receive ministry, but they are needs nonetheless that open the possibility for spiritual engagement and healing.

EFFECTIVE KINGDOM LEADERS HELP CONNECT THE DOTS BETWEEN VOLUNTEERS' EFFORTS AND THE LARGER VISION OF GOD'S KINGDOM.

I saw a great example of serving volunteers this way some years ago while visiting a community work project sponsored and managed by a faith group in New York City. The project involved over two hundred volunteers from one local company that, in a single day, painted a large urban high school facility in Manhattan. The volunteers had a blast doing something for the community with their coworkers. But it also provided them with a chance to brush up against the kingdom.

The project manager (a young millennial) used the lunch gathering not only to bless the pizza, but also to pray a blessing over the assembled volunteers, right after thanking them for their hard work and "painting" a picture of what their labor meant to the school and students. All the volunteers were made to feel special and more connected to their service and to something larger than themselves. No one stormed out of the room offended at being blessed (or refused the pizza!).

Effective kingdom leaders help connect the dots between volunteers' efforts and the larger vision of God's kingdom. This intentionality paves the way for further spiritual reflection and conversation. When people realize they're acting as conspirators with God to help others live better lives, it often accelerates their spiritual journey. Their efforts have greater meaning.

3. Failure to honor the efforts of volunteers appropriately. The Dream Center in Phoenix hosts their team of hundreds of volunteers for dinner one night each month. This isn't because their volunteers are all food-challenged (though some are!). They do it so they can demonstrate their appreciation for their work. These effective kingdom leaders accomplish this not only through preparing and serving a delicious meal to these workers but by what they do after the meal. They tell stories. Stories of people whose lives they've touched and improved—and even transformed. These stories aren't all told by the Center staff; they're often told by ministry recipients themselves.

Nothing honors volunteers more than to know they made a difference in someone's life. At some level, this was their motivation to get involved initially and to offer their service. These reminders of the *why* their service matters mobilize and motivate hundreds of people to continue to volunteer their time, money, and effort to the Center's work.

Kingdom collaborators demonstrate a bias toward action. They marry vision with action. They don't engage in activity for the sake of appearing busy. (Maybe you've seen the bumper snicker: "Jesus is coming soon. . . . Look busy!")

Kingdom leaders are urgently pursuing a better world in which having to do something and having something to do come together where vision and action meet. When this marriage occurs, all parties—those delivering and those receiving ministry—grow in their awareness of God's kingdom.

DEVELOPING

PEOPLE ARE BUILT TO LAST. Forever. The same can't be said of companies, countries, churches, or even the cosmos. But people created by God in his image are fashioned for eternity. This amazing truth means that every person we encounter in this life is on a journey that's just getting started.

God's preferred future for human beings is that we spend our eternity with him in his kingdom. His engagement with us centers on the hope of our entering his kingdom and experiencing the life he intends for us. He has gone to extraordinary efforts to create access for us to this future, including a personal visit and sojourn on the planet. Jesus battled and conquered evil forces that seek to thwart God's intentions for humanity. The core of the gospel (good news) that he lived and shared celebrates the reality of God's kingdom. His redemptive sacrifice secured access to this kingdom.

Kingdom collaborators prioritize the developing of people in light of humanity's destiny. Their work includes preparing people for eternity. But it also involves helping people live as God intends for them here and now in all aspects of their lives—physical, emotional, relational, financial. Jesus called this abundant life (John 10:10 NKJV). And he meant it to be enjoyed on earth.

This concern for people's holistic well-being means kingdom leaders search for ways to improve the lives of the people in their constellation of relationships: family members, coworkers, peers, friends, neighbors. The great thrill for these leaders is to observe the positive development of people in all these spheres of their life and leadership. This commitment also influences these leaders' scorecards. They want to note and celebrate positive impact and growth in others' personal development. In short, kingdom leaders shape a people-development culture around them.

Dave Rocheleau is a perfect example of what we're talking about. He's a professor at the University of South Carolina here in Columbia, where I live, and is acting as the director of graduate studies for the Department of Mechanical Engineering. Dave is also a Jesus-follower, looking for ways to have a positive impact in the academic world where he spends most of his time.

Recently Dave heard the director of a local after-school program serving two inner-city elementary schools express the hope that he could eventually secure a 3D printer in an effort to expose his kids to some high-tech devices. Dave immediately offered the director access to the university's state-of-the-art machine and proposed a joint project. As an option for their final coursework, he would give his students the choice of mentoring one of the elementary students through designing and printing an artifact. Almost every one of Dave's students volunteered to participate—so many that they had to create a lottery to determine who would get to do the special project.

A dozen older elementary school children were each assigned to an engineering student who came to the after-school site a couple of times to work with them in designing their artifact. Then the kids were taken one afternoon to the university's engineering school to receive the object they had designed. Their visit included a tour of the school's labs, where all the big machines are housed, leading up to the main event: seeing the large 3D printer and being presented with their artifact.

The student mentors went through the tour with them and then had the privilege of making the artifact presentation to them. Then the students journeyed over to the student center in the heart of the campus, where they had dinner in the food court.

Keep in mind that these young students come from homes and neighborhoods where few people graduate from high school, much less attend college. None of them had ever set foot on this university campus, even though it's only a few miles from where they live. One can imagine the possibilities that this project created in the minds of these children. On top of the STEM support, this project may have inspired them to dream that they can complete a college education. Perhaps their entire life trajectory was altered!

Dave didn't pursue the project with a one-dimensional approach for his students: just deliver an artifact to an elementary school kid. As part of the project grade for his students, he required that they write a reflection paper on their experience of mentoring. Obviously Dave wanted them to think not only about their impact on the children, but also the impact of the children on their own lives. Below are a few of their observations. Keep in mind that these are undergraduate engineering students, not given to reflection and gushing emotions:

> It gave me the opportunity to build a relationship with a kid who may feel like he doesn't have an opportunity to attend a university like USC.

> When attending class, one doesn't normally have the opportunity to make a potential change in a child's life.

> The project gave us a chance to make a child happy, and that alone was the best outcome of the entire project.

> The memories of this project will hold a very special place in my undergraduate experience at USC.

Dave created an experience that afforded people (both elementary and college students alike) new insights into their personal development as well as the awareness of others' life experiences. This is the essence of people-development dynamics: helping people become people. Dave's kingdom leadership was expressed in his creating an opportunity for people's lives to be enriched and enhanced—and maybe even transformed.

In this chapter, we examine how kingdom collaborators create environments that support people development. They typically influence the shaping of their organizational culture. So the first part of our discussion identifies some key elements of a people-development culture. My hope is to inform kingdom leaders of specific components that can enhance where they have influence, whether it's on a work team at the office or in a volunteer ministry, with their co-workers in their local department or on a multinational corporate level.

The second part of this chapter focuses specifically on considering discipleship to be people development. God has designs for every part of a disciple's life. Therefore, efforts that help that disciple grow—spiritually, emotionally, relationally, whatever—are discipleship efforts. Since many reading this book have church responsibilities that include some stewardship of congregational development and disciple-making processes, this section includes a list of questions we should be asking as we think about our discipleship (people-development efforts) efforts.

A final part of the chapter aims to help kingdom leaders (no matter where they're assigned) to engage people in conversations that focus on their development. It offers questions that leaders can use to invite people into this dialogue about themselves and their personal growth. Exploring these questions helps people connect the dots of what God is up to in their life.

CRAFTING A CULTURE THAT SUPPORTS PEOPLE DEVELOPMENT

Perhaps it goes without saying, but the key for creating a culture that supports people development is the conscious and constant awareness that developing people *is the point*. Unless this outcome rises to the level of a shared conviction across the organization, it will probably succumb to other corporate activity. Substitute agendas—like program development and participation, or organizational advancement, for instance—too easily creep in. Adopting people development as the main agenda shapes leadership efforts and corporate scorecards to support and measure that outcome.

People-development cultures reflect some essential architectural components in their design. Kingdom conspirators look for ways to incorporate these signature core elements into their environment.

Customization. Helping people grow into their own skin requires a customized approach. The printing press made possible mass standardization, a development that gave rise to the modern industrial world. Now the digital information revolution makes possible mass customization. People who are used to customizing their ringtones, their online shopping purchases, and their entertainment options also want to customize their growth path. While certain categories of personal development are always appropriate for everyone (relationships, spiritual formation, emotional/psychological health, etc.), each person's needs are peculiar to him.

Approaches addressing these areas that will prove most effective also require accommodation to individual styles and preferences. Jesus demonstrated this in the different approaches he took with people. He connected at a point of growth. For the rich young ruler, it was to sell everything he had (not a commandment for everyone). His instruction for the woman at the well to introduce him to her husband was a unique and personal way to begin a discussion about her spiritual journey. We have no other recorded case where he began his interactions with people with this request.

Cross-generational interaction. Wisdom for life's various challenges is distributed across generational cohorts. Younglings need the insights and life skills archived in older generations. Seniors need reverse mentoring by members of younger generations to help them navigate the new world created by the rise of digital technology. People-development cultures combat generational silos by finding ways to increase cross-generational engagement. In their programming, especially in their work and serving projects, they create "white space" fellowship opportunities. These spaces are times and places in organizational life that foster generational interactions that aren't agenda-driven.

One business owner who had several hundred employees allowed the workers to customize their offices with the furniture, art, or decorations of their choice but didn't allow a coffee pot in any office. Workers were required to spend their coffee breaks in the company's cafeteria (a magnificently warm space—with good coffee!) so that relationships could be more easily and naturally established and nourished.

Growing through service. People-development cultures understand that people don't just grow *into* service; they grow *through* service. The Scriptures abound with insightful narratives that illustrate the dynamic of growing through service. Moses' objections that he wasn't equipped to lead the Exodus were swatted away by God, who told him that he would give him what he needed to pull it off once he began. Jesus sent his disciples out on mission early in his ministry as part of their training (Matthew 10, Mark 6, Luke 10). The New Testament would be a lot shorter and the church much smaller had Paul not grown through his role in serving the young movement of Jesus-followers.

Serving others has long been underutilized as an opportunity to support growth and development in the lives of the ones who serve, not just the ones being served. Many people discover things about themselves in these situations: what they bring to the table in terms of talent, what personal biases and prejudices they carry (sometimes unknowingly), what they experienced that they hope to experience again, and what they hope never to repeat. Giving people assignments and opportunities to serve in areas beyond their comfort zones and usual environments often can be very effective at uncovering personal insights.

Life-centric coaching. Kingdom leaders strive to create an environment where people can ask for and receive help with their concerns. What's going on in people's lives is the background noise playing in their heads and hearts all the time. Their circumstances and situations impact their work performance, relational health, physical condition, and every other aspect of their lives.

Helping people make greater meaning out of the life they're living requires a coaching ethos to be in place. Coaches help people know how to debrief their life experiences, allowing them to connect the dots of the insights they glean.

WHAT'S GOING ON IN PEOPLE'S LIVES IS THE BACKGROUND NOISE PLAYING IN THEIR HEADS AND HEARTS ALL THE TIME.

These discoveries in turn help them shift perspective(s) and behavior(s).

The assumption that people learn most of what they know through curriculum or class settings—a belief tenaciously held—has shaped much of our educational and spiritual formation design, and it needs to be reexamined. Teaching people truths and then sending them out to apply them rarely produces life transformation. What we know is that most people learn through *experience* of some kind, whether positive or negative. Mentoring and coaching through life-on-life relationships (like Jesus did with his disciples) produces much more significant personal growth and development.

Relational. Undergirding all these key characteristics of a people-development culture is a prevailing bias toward building and sustaining relationships. Kingdom leaders understand that building a relationship-friendly environment increases the possibilities and likelihood that people will invest in each other. An environment of trust, transparency, and truth telling fosters strong relationships. The weight limit of a culture's capacity to help people grow and develop is determined by the strength of the relationships in that environment.

The latest research into identifying the important factors that allow people to overcome addictions and change their life trajectory reveals the power of having a significant community around them. Jesus created a community of disciples that would become leaders of the kingdom movement he established. The birth of the church occurred as they remained in community with each other after Jesus' ascension.

The transformation of their lives, supported by this community, was the seminal dynamic verifying that the kingdom had been unleashed.

Bottom line, the people who live and work around kingdom conspirators are better people because of it. That's because they've been engaged intentionally for their personal growth and development.

SHAPING A DISCIPLESHIP CULTURE

Let's apply this people-development culture to congregational or church life. Two reasons prompt this discussion. First, many have responsibilities in this arena. Second, too many disciple-making efforts use the wrong scorecard: participation rather than maturation. In other words, we keep people busy coming to church activities, studying, meeting, socializing. But are the people involved in doing all this really growing as followers of Jesus? Are they becoming viral kingdom agents? Our gut (and a lot of surveys) say no. The evidence of the lack of kingdom impact begs us to investigate how our discipleship efforts can be more transformative.

When I consult with groups that want to consider how they can improve discipleship (people development), I ask them to ponder some strategic questions.

1. Why are we reluctant to examine our assumptions about discipleship? Part of the answer to this question lies in the fear of having to confront two prevailing myths. The first admission we would have to make is that a compartmentalized life (fostered by viewing discipleship as a church program engaging just a slice of our lives) supports church-as-institution through its consumer orientation. Discipleship that's offered as an optional part of church programming fails to provide genuine spiritual formation, instead substituting religious activity for life transformation.

The second myth closely tracks with the first. Information by itself—absent experience and reflection—does not have the power to transform. Yet we continue to offer more and more Bible studies and curriculum, pretending that by engaging in these we're creating Jesus-followers who live as viral kingdom agents. Behind these myths lurks an even more telling reason why we continue to double down on approaches that create religious consumers but not disciples. Most pastors in America admit to never having been discipled themselves. So they have no idea how to replicate the process.

They continue to do only what they know how to do (teach classes, create educational programs) and call it discipleship.

2. Does our thinking about discipleship begin with a program or with people? Since this chapter is about developing people, you can probably guess my take on this. Please don't hear what I am *not* saying. We obviously need and use programs for lots of good reasons, including developing people. However, people—not programs—*are the point*!

If we begin by designing discipleship programs, we end up focusing on marketing church activities and recruiting people into supporting the programs. As labor-intensive as it is, our discipling effort should be built around a person, tailored to his or her needs, life rhythms, passions, etc. One or more programs may provide an appropriate and important component of a discipleship strategy for that person. This causes us to focus on our starting point, revealing whether we are in the people business or the church-program business.

3. What is the underlying narrative of our view of discipleship? This narrative is critical, whether it's expressed or just assumed, because it shapes the approach as well as determines the goal of our discipling efforts. Two prominent narratives guide many discipleship approaches and goals: people need to be fixed, and commitment to Jesus is represented by one's commitment to the church. A kingdom narrative would be expressed something like this: developing people into viral kingdom agents, or helping people become the people God intends them to be, or helping people follow Jesus by seeking first the kingdom of God. These kingdom story lines require different approaches and goals than the church-centric model.

4. Do we need to turn people into church people first before we connect with them for discipleship? The answer to this question reveals whether our understanding of discipleship is kingdom-centric or church-centric. If our position is the latter, we primarily plan how to help people grow once they're connected to the church. In a kingdom paradigm, we adopt the approach that we can disciple everyone in our constellation of influence: those we touch through our members' relationships, those we serve through our community engagement efforts, those who visit our website but who will never visit our campus. In doing this, we have an opportunity and a responsibility to develop as people created in the image of God.

5. Are we thinking of delivering discipling as part of our "regularly scheduled programming," or can we allow people to customize their engagement? This question directly reflects the element of customization we've already identified as a critical factor in creating a people-development culture. Before the advent of DVR technology, TV shows could be watched only during broadcast times. Now most Americans record their cable TV shows to watch them at their own convenience. Do we have similar options in our discipleship offerings? Can we think of approaching discipleship processes with asynchronous/ubiquitous (anytime/anywhere) aspects? And can we allow for differences in how people grow? Different cognitive styles respond differently to learning approaches. While the classroom model works for some, many prefer experiential learning. For them, we need to incorporate intentional spiritual experiences into their discipleship path (mission trips, service opportunities, retreats, etc.).

6. Can we move from a mostly didactic discipleship approach to one that focuses on personal discovery? One congregation I've worked with uses the following description for its discipling ministry: "Great information regarding Christ leads to transforming imitation of Christ." Not necessarily! This assumption perfectly describes why this church (and many others that believe this narrative but don't declare it) puts the majority of its discipling efforts into classes, curriculum, and church-centric activity. This transition requires that we commit to becoming more of a coaching culture, allowing people frequent and regular opportunities to debrief their lives, to connect the dots, to discover what God is up to in them and in the people and situations around them. An approach focused on discovery would have impact across the board, from sermon takeaways to how we conduct elder meetings to the content of our ministry team conversations to how we develop leaders for ministry.

7. How do we help people know they're developing as disciples? When participation is the goal for church members (as it most often is in the program-driven church), keeping track of progress simply means charting attendance and support for congregational or organizational activities. But deciding to pursue discipleship as a people-development agenda begs for another scorecard. My suggestions in my consultative practice are always made in a particular context but generally involve similar components: giving people the opportunity to declare their growth areas, helping them work with others to develop a path to address these issues, and giving people the chance to report and celebrate their progress and/or declare new areas for development.

8. Are we willing to determine congregational success in discipleship based on the reported growth of the people in our ministry rather than on their participation in our programs? This approach would mean that we ask people to report on their development. I frequently ask pastors, "How many better marriages do you have in your church than you did last year?"

These spiritual leaders usually look at me as if I have one eye in the middle of my forehead. "We don't know that," they usually respond.

I say, "Why not?"

The next question from them usually is "How would we know that?"

I reply, "You ask them!"

I contend that married people are generally concerned about how their marriage is going and have a pretty good idea of whether or not it needs help or is improving, is in a crisis mode or progressing positively. Similar inquiries could be made of parents about their relationships with their kids, or of people about their life satisfaction, relational health, etc. In other words, people deal every day with the issues of life (kingdom issues). And they would report on how they're doing if we asked. So, why don't we? We aren't shy about asking them for more money, more time, more energy to keep our church programs going. I'm amazed that people have annual physicals, twice-a-year teeth cleanings, and routine job reviews, yet we never talk with congregants about their life development (unless they're in a crisis).

My hope is that if you have leadership responsibility in a congregation, you use these questions to prompt some evaluation and creative discussions about your discipleship efforts. If you lean toward a kingdom bias in your thinking, these questions can provide an opportunity for you and your team to incorporate a greater kingdom perspective (with greater life-centric dimensions) into your people-development processes.

PREPARING PEOPLE FOR LIFE

As I've mentioned before, I approach the future in a *preparedness* modality rather than having just a planning approach. Planning generally takes what we know and pushes it into the future. The problem is, we can't predict the future. Many of the things that impact our lives happen outside our control (economic downturns, political upheavals, our genes, just to name a few). The same is true for organizations; most of what impacts an organization happens outside the organization. So a planning modality that deals only with what we already know is limited; right off the bat, it limits our ability to be ready for what's next. I often use an analogy drawn from surfing. Surfers don't plan waves, but they're ready when waves come. Similarly, people and organizations need to be prepared to ride the waves that come their way.

SURFERS DON'T PLAN WAVES, BUT THEY'RE READY WHEN WAVES COME. SIMILARLY, PEOPLE AND ORGANIZATIONS NEED TO BE PREPARED TO RIDE THE WAVES THAT COME THEIR WAY.

Five elements compose the core essence of a preparedness modality: vision, values, results, strengths, and learning. These elements can scale up or down, meaning they're the same for a person as for a small group or a large organization.

In my coaching and consulting, I've developed a simple set of questions to explore and discuss preparedness for the life

God wants for my clients. These are questions you as a kingdom leader can use, whatever your assignment. They help to frame a conversation so you can discuss a person's life preparedness. You can engage coworkers with them, professional colleagues, family members, neighbors, people in your church small group—anyone who allows you to speak into their life. You may even ask *yourself* these questions. I have used them in all these contexts—yes, even with myself.

▼ *Vision.* What does your life's next chapter involve? *Or* what's next for you? This question allows you to explore both challenges and opportunities for the future. Often people can't be specific with their response, but their answer reveals what they see as their next life challenge or opportunity. We then explore various options or possibilities for meeting each of them. The goal of this question goes beyond coming up with an answer. Wrestling with the answer helps make the future more tangible and less fuzzy, more friendly, and less foreboding. I want them to envision the preferred future God has for them.

▼ *Values.* What behaviors will support this future? People often need help identifying the behaviors they need to abandon or alter that continue to sabotage the preferred future they envision. These behaviors sometimes are hard-to-break habits. Conversely, many people need help determining the behaviors that will help them achieve the vision of the next chapter of their lives. This includes new ways of thinking and acting that become positive habits and responses to circumstances and situations.

▼ *Results.* How will you know when you're making progress? This is the scorecard question. People need to know they're moving forward—or not! By teasing out some mile markers, specifying some results that would show positive growth and development, a person builds motivation and celebration into his or her developmental path. These results need to be both incremental and long-term.

▼ *Strengths.* What do I bring to the table? A sober assessment of what we have going for us can help us know the best way to approach our various endeavors, including the challenges and opportunities of the next chapter. This approach to personal development has gained significant traction over the past two decades. All of us have talents and abilities that are packed into our life backpack by the God who created us on purpose for a purpose. Our lives are mission trips. God has equipped us for our journeys. Our skills, talents, and abilities hold great clues as to what we have been sent to do. This means that our best shot at making our best contribution is for us to get better at what we're already good at. We don't ignore our weaknesses; we manage them. But we build on our strengths.

▼ *Learning.* What do I need to learn? As the saying goes, people don't know what they don't know. We can shrink that gap significantly by carefully thinking through what we *know* we need to learn. This may include new skills, new insights, new ways of thinking, new ways of working, new ways of behaving. Adding these new items to our lives frequently involves some significant *unlearning* in terms of our mind and habits. The unlearning curve often proves steeper than the learning curve.

Those who explore these five questions and can articulate some answers, even partial ones, place themselves in a posture of being prepared for the future God has in mind for them.

God created the whole universe in six days but has set aside the rest of eternity for people to develop. Developing creatures made in God's image claim his attention in his eternal kingdom, so kingdom collaborators believe it should be their focus on earth.

CURIOSITY

I MET DON "DOC" CLIFTON in a weeklong leadership work-shop he hosted almost twenty years ago. He was one of the youngest people I knew at the time, though he was in his mid-seventies. Insatiably curious, he was piloting the company he owned into greater engagement with leadership development in all sectors of the culture—government, business, education, healthcare, not-for-profit, entertainment—you name it. (Other participants in the workshop with me included people from Disney, State Farm, the Army Corps of Engineers, the Robert Wood Johnson Foundation, Stryker Instruments, along with a few Protestant clergy.) We met in Lincoln, Nebraska, at the company's then-headquarters. You may have heard of the outfit. It's called the Gallup Organization.

Don and I engaged in projects on several occasions during a few years that followed until his much-too-early departure from this world. The project that had captured his greatest curiosity and the company's attention was just going public in those days. It was called the Gallup StrengthsFinder (now CliftonStrengths), an online instrument designed to give people immediate feedback on their top strengths, along with strategies for building on their talent.

Even if you haven't taken this particular survey (I recommend it for all my clients), you've probably been exposed to strengths-based thinking and development. If you have, that's because Don Clifton pursued his passion to help people improve their lives and personal performance by knowing and developing their strengths.

Don acquired the Gallup company after serving as one of its major vendors, helping Gallup with its well-known polling operation. Subsequently he moved the company into management and leadership training based on his determination to help people understand themselves better. His immersion in the field of education (including a doctorate and serving as a professor in educational psychology at the University of Nebraska) convinced him that personal development efforts (like formal education and professional training) need to be customized to the individual and focused on helping people get better at what they're already good at. This approach, he would often say, provided people their best chance at making their best contribution. (Just to be clear, Don said we can't ignore our weaknesses, but we *manage* them while we build on our strengths.)

Twenty years later, this strength-biased insight has gained widespread traction. That wasn't the case when Don began to wage his campaign for strengths-based development. His approach went against the grain of the typical developmental approaches of his day. Managerial and leadership training back then helped people to identify their weaknesses—both personal and professional—and to focus on making improvement in those areas. It was a pathology-based approach. Topflight training agendas often included psychological and emotional assessments and relied on observational feedback loops and reflections designed to identify and eradicate personal weaknesses.

Don rightly contended that a language had to be created to support a shift into strengths-based development. Over two million interviews of leaders and managers were in Gallup's database. Don assigned his researchers the task of doing a meta-analysis of the data to develop a taxonomy of strengths that gave birth to the StrengthsFinder instrument. The precision of its descriptions has given us a way to communicate specific information about ourselves. Many leaders I correspond with include their StrengthsFinder set of descriptors in their email signature.

Curiosity may have killed the cat, but it enlivened Don Clifton. The landscape of personal and professional development was altered by a man who was curious and who believed that people are motivated by their curiosity to discover something positive about themselves. As another example of his inquisitiveness, during his stint as president of the American Psychological Association, he convened the group's first conference focused on happiness. He explained to the delegates that forty years of focusing on depression and other issues had left unexplored the topic of well-being.

Of course, Don was already hard at work in this area. He unveiled some early findings around the discovery that people have emotional and psychological "set points" that provide them their sense of well-being. His thinking and inquiries gave rise to Gallup's Well-Being Survey, now conducted globally—a project that came to fruition after Don's death.

Don was a kingdom leader as a churchgoing Methodist. He and I had several discussions about the philosophical underpinnings of his approach to people's development being rooted in biblical theology and perspective. Don established a Faith Communities team at Gallup to explore how a strengths-based approach could help church leaders identify congregational strengths and build on them.

At the time of his death, he and I were engaged in exploring how church leaders and congregations could benefit from focusing on their individual design. We were particularly interested in helping church leaders address the emerging trends in ministerial burnout by shifting their emphasis from comparing themselves with others to focusing on identifying and developing their unique contributions to the body of Christ and to the community. Our last set of correspondence centered on feedback he gave me after he spent part of a weekend reviewing some material I'd sent him on this topic, a weekend spent in "learning," he said as he detailed his new insights. Only a strong curiosity would move a world leader to spend his weekend that way.

I've rehearsed my too-brief, highly significant relationship with Don Clifton for one reason: I want to give you an example of how a kingdom leader can have enormous influence when he is driven by curiosity. Don's eyes literally twinkled whenever he talked about the discoveries he and his team were making. His findings and insights have positively impacted a myriad of lives by inviting people into self-discovery and development in a way that aligns them with God's design in them.

In this chapter, we take a look at the operation of curiosity in kingdom leaders. Our exploration includes a discussion of lifelong learning—and lifelong unlearning—that paves the way for it. We also identify some key ways kingdom leaders nurture their curiosity, through both the people they surround themselves with and the environment they create to keep their curiosity flourishing.

LIFELONG LEARNING

When he was eighty, Peter Drucker gave an interview in which one of the questions was whether what he taught then was different from what he'd taught ten years earlier. Drucker's response revealed why he was such a powerful thought leader in business management and strategy. "I'm not teaching *anything* I was teaching ten years ago!"

While many people are working from their old notes by age seventy, he refused to blow the dust off his lectures and coast on his reputation and past insight. His continuous revision of his teaching content lined up with one of his important pieces of advice to companies: practice systematic abandonment and reinvent routinely.

Perhaps Drucker's Episcopalian background tenderized him to the leadership challenges of the faith sector. He felt that the rise of the "large pastoral church" as he called it (today we call it the megachurch) was the most important sociological phenomenon of the last half of the twentieth century in America. He made this observation late in his career as he continued to study the shifts underway in American culture. He sometimes wrote for and spoke to church leaders, bringing his considerable management acumen and cultural insights to bear on the unique challenge of leading nonprofit organizations.

Drucker kept fresh, current, and insightful throughout his life because he was curious. His curiosity fueled his lifelong learning. Contrast Drucker's learning posture to a leader who stubbornly refuses to acknowledge his need to revisit some of his ideas. In recent years, I've watched a pastor inflict his outmoded ideas, toxic leadership style, and stale approaches on a congregation that was vibrant before suffering through seven years of his bad leadership. When very early in his pastorate attendance and even membership decreased (people left in unprecedented numbers), the pastor started trying everything he knew.

The sad truth was that what he knew was old and useless. It had already failed him once, leading to an early retirement from the pastorate, followed by an unsuccessful attempt at establishing a consulting practice. Unfortunately, when he reentered pastoral ministry, he dusted off his old notes rather than approach his new stewardship by learning the church, community, and cultural challenges he faced in the new assignment. He ran the church into the ground and retired again at age seventy, too late for him and probably too late for the congregation to recover.

I sometimes ask leaders, "When is the last time Jesus changed your mind about something?" Their answer reveals the vibrancy of their relationship with him. People who occupy integral parts of my life shape and reshape my opinions about issues in the world on a regular basis. And after thirty-five years of marriage, my wife still changes my mind all the time!

My follow-up question provides a clue about the leader's learning (and unlearning) aptitude: "When was the last time you changed your mind about something that significantly impacted your life or work?"

Kingdom leaders are lifelong learners. Probably no other single attribute correlates more closely with whether or not they finish well. On the other hand, leaders who "stale out" wind up limiting their influence. In the worst cases, they do kingdom damage. Most of the rest of this chapter gives clues about how a leader sustains lifelong learning.

I SOMETIMES ASK LEADERS, "WHEN IS THE LAST TIME JESUS CHANGED YOUR MIND ABOUT SOMETHING?"

LIFELONG UNLEARNING

Lifelong learning demands lifelong *unlearning*. Leaders not only need to pay attention to new competencies, skills, and insights, they also have to figure out what elements they need to abandon in order to maintain or enhance their leadership effectiveness. Items needing to undergo revision may include the leader's way of thinking about certain issues, her biases and perspectives, long-held ideas about how the world operates, and the role of the leader herself in this new world. The unlearning curve can prove steeper than the learning curve!

The apostle Paul is a perfect example of a leader who underwent significant unlearning to become an effective kingdom leader for the early Christian movement. His contributions are many. But in terms of his learning, two particular areas come to mind: his early formation of trinitarian theology and the missional zeal he stamped into the church.

Like every Jew, Paul learned the Shema early on and repeated it often: "Hear, O Israel: the LORD our God, the LORD is one" (Deuteronomy 6:4). Israel's radical monotheism—originating from the life and experience of Abraham—was an important development in the ancient world. Before Abraham, gods were nationalistic or tribal. When a Bedouin moved from one place to another, he packed up his gods and moved them to the new location, where he then set them back out. Abraham's story played out differently at this point. In the Old Testament narrative, God informed Abraham that he (God) was packing him up to move him to a new location. God was already familiar with the new destination, because it was *already there*.

This encounter provided the roots of Israel's growing commitment to one God. Early Old Testament accounts posture Israel's God as superior to other gods. By the time Paul had received his instruction at the hands of the Pharisees, Israel had long ago adopted a radical monotheism that held that there is *only one* God.

Imagine the disruption of Paul's theology in his Damascus Road experience. First, he had an encounter with a divine being on the road into town. Jesus clearly identified himself to him and subsequently convinced Paul of his claims. Immediately after his blindness, conversion, and baptism, Paul "began to preach in the synagogues that Jesus is the Son of God" (Acts 9:20). This message flew squarely in the face of his rabbinical training (and didn't set well with his former religious colleagues either). On top of dealing with Jesus, Paul also was introduced to the Holy Spirit (Acts 9:17).

No wonder Paul soon retreated to the desert for a couple of years. He had to put his head on straight again! His theological framework had been rocked at its doctrinal core. Paul had to wrap his considerably bright mind around the new reality he had encountered and was experiencing. It would take the church almost three centuries to figure out how to express its trinitarian formula, but it was built on the foundation principally laid by Paul. His understanding of God as Three-in-One could be accommodated in his thinking only because he was willing to unlearn what he knew. He had to make room for a new expression of God in the world.

The Pharisees had expected God to show up with a world-changing agenda—but not like it happened. As a Pharisee, Paul had been taught to work for the coming of the Messiah. Pharisees believed that God would send the Messiah once a critical mass of people was obeying enough of the law (hence the Pharisee obsession with keeping the sabbath). Further, the coming of the Messiah would usher in the messianic kingdom, centered in Israel. The establishment and unveiling of the messianic era would be occasioned by a bodily resurrection of the just (law keepers). These tenets comprised the hope and central dogma of Pharisee eschatological doctrine.

Given this understanding of what Paul had been taught and firmly believed, consider the chain of thoughts that were triggered by his Damascus Road experience: He meets a resurrected being, signaling that God had sent the Messiah and inaugurated the establishment of the messianic kingdom. Jesus identifies himself as that Messiah. Paul suddenly realizes he is opposing the work of God by persecuting Jesus and his followers. Furthermore, God had sent Jesus as an act of grace, not as a reward for Jewish faithfulness to the law.

Paul's emphasis on the gospel of grace is rooted in these disruptive realities. To his credit, when his entire theological construct was challenged and proven incorrect, Paul didn't blindly (pun intended) follow his old convictions. Instead, he zealously followed the implications of new revelation.

Another sign of Paul's unlearning shows up in the missionary DNA he infused into the early Christian movement. Again, this development ran counter to his training as a Pharisee. First-century Pharisaic Judaism had grown exclusive and inward-focused. The daily prayer of devout Pharisees began with expressing thanks to God that they hadn't been born a Gentile, a slave, or a woman. Paul expressly repudiated this perspective early in his thinking. Writing to the Galatians, he said, "There is neither Jew nor Gentile, neither slave nor free, nor is there male and female, for you are all one in Christ Jesus" (Galatians 3:28). Paul demonstrated his new values throughout his journeys and in his significant interactions with Gentiles, slaves, and women for the rest of his ministry.

Paul's willingness to unlearn old biases and prejudices paved the way for an inclusive Christian movement. He argued for this position consistently, beginning with church leaders in Jerusalem. He even famously challenged the apostle Peter when he felt Peter's actions (pulling back from eating publicly with Gentiles) threatened the emerging character of the movement (Galatians 2:11-14). Paul's position was far ahead of the thinking of his day in Jewish religious circles. Because he was willing to unlearn his old perspective, he laid the groundwork for others throughout history to build on what it means to be one in Christ.

Like Paul, kingdom leaders are willing to unlearn what they know or think they know. As they encounter God's work in the world, in the people around them, and in themselves, they remain open to learning—and to unlearning. Driven by curiosity, they don't want to miss what God is up to by clinging to old ideas and perspectives that blind them to current realities. This attitude requires humility on their part. There is always more to learn, and sometimes unlearning paves the way for it.

LIKE PAUL, KINGDOM LEADERS ARE WILLING TO UNLEARN WHAT THEY KNOW OR THINK THEY KNOW.

A current example of this unlearning-learning dynamic is the shift underway from a church-centric to kingdom-centric thinking. This is as big a shift theologically as was the move from a Ptolemaic universe to a Copernican one in cosmology and from a Newtonian to a quantum world in physics. A lot of unlearning is going on right now!

We are unlearning that the church is the primary mission of God in the world (the kingdom is). We are unlearning that Jesus came to establish a religion and an institution to support it (he came to reveal the kingdom). We are unlearning that God is most at work in the church (the kingdom is most at work in the world in all domains of human activity). We are unlearning that spiritual leadership exists primarily to work for the success of the church as an institution (kingdom leadership is found in all cultural domains to promote life as God intends).

Like Paul, spiritual leaders willing to undergo such unlearning are finding that the greatest pushback to their new learning comes from those who are firmly rooted in the old world, who can't tolerate such thinking because it threatens the system that supports their identity and activity.

Unlearning often requires significant courage on the part of the leader, especially if it challenges existing norms. This courage can be fueled by curiosity strong enough to overcome the tendency to shrink back from the unfamiliar or disruptive work of God. Kingdom leaders take the risk—and follow this curiosity—because they want to partner with God in what he's doing in the world.

THE COMPANY YOU KEEP

Many of us grew up hearing the maxim "We are known by the company we keep." Kingdom leaders decide they *know* by the company they keep. They frequently include three kinds of people in their constellation of relationships who help to fuel their curiosity.

First, kingdom leaders seek out people who *aren't like them*. They maintain significant diversity in their relationships, both in the workplace as well as in their personal and social connections. The diversity can stretch across a wide spectrum of categories: different ethnicities, generational cohorts, cultures, social backgrounds, cognitive styles, worldviews, and more.

This isn't practicing diversity for diversity's sake. Kingdom leaders need the benefits of diversity. Intentional diversity automatically and naturally forces discussions and considerations that provide the leader with knowledge and insight he otherwise wouldn't have. Maintaining and cultivating relationships with people of diverse backgrounds helps the leader avoid the tunnel vision that afflicts those who insist that everyone around them think like they do, like what they like, and see the world as they see it. Diversity supports the likelihood of a robust workplace, an interesting social life, and a home and personal environment that welcomes differences of opinion. Curious people not only tolerate diversity, they go after it!

Second, curious leaders welcome people who *challenge them*. Challenges stretch the leader in a variety of ways: intellectually, spiritually, and even in terms of personal development or leadership capacity and competence. A leader may have mentors or long-time acquaintances or friends who fill this role, or she may hire coaches to introduce some of this element into her life or work. Curious leaders always have someone who provides this element for their development.

Third, kingdom leaders find people who are *interesting*. Maybe those people have life experiences that intrigue the leader. Perhaps they have access to other leaders' opinions and agendas that the leader wants to know. Their knowledge base or background may pique the leader's interest for any number of reasons. Or maybe their personality simply draws the leader to them, and they provide an element of fun to the leader's life.

Consider the menagerie of people Jesus kept around him: contemplative John, brash Peter, volatile Simon, prosperous Lazarus, devoted Mary, task-driven Martha, shrewd Judas. We do well to follow the example of the ultimate kingdom leader by opening our lives to a wide range of people both for what they bring into the kingdom and for their vistas of knowledge, insight, and perspective that raise our curiosity.

FEEDING YOUR CURIOSITY

Curiosity can suffer from malnutrition. Leaders who want to keep exploring and discovering ideas and insights that fuel their creative energy realize how important it is to feed their inquisitive side. How leaders go about this depends on many variables: their learning style, available resources, geographical location, access to people and places, as well as their particular interests and the work they're engaged in. No matter the differing elements for different leaders, *people, places*, and *experiences* serve as nutrient sources for maintaining an environment that supports a kingdom leader's inquisitiveness.

The leader needs access to people who stimulate her thinking. We've already discussed this, but I want to drive home the point that much of a leader's development depends on the people and relationships she intentionally pursues. Ideally her access to stimulating people can be enjoyed on a routine and natural basis. If the leader creates intersections with people who fill this need, they will. These interfaces may include ongoing education or attending conferences and seminars.

The leader may also hire a coach or employ a consultant. Some leaders hire people like me for a day every year or two just so we can spend time together dreaming, processing their experiences and what they learned from them, figuring out next steps—whatever that leader is working on or needs to talk about. Every curious leader I know reads—many voraciously—to access the minds and thoughts of stimulating people. They read books, blogs, articles, papers, journals, and magazines that cover a wide spectrum of interests, not just their field of practice.

Special places can contribute to sustaining a leader's curiosity. Many leaders find that travel enlarges their world. Contact with other cultures provides great insight into God's engagement with the world by how he has revealed himself to people of those cultures. These exposures heighten the kingdom leader's appreciation for the many ways God works in and among people.

Kingdom leaders often seek out places that can be informative for their own development as a leader or for a particular endeavor they're pursuing. Just today I helped a pastor plan his five-week sabbatical to accelerate his expertise in community development. He's on the front end of putting together a multidomain coalition in his city to tackle big issues in education, healthcare, and poverty, so he wanted recommendations on places he could visit to see work already underway. He'll pick up a wealth of new ideas and operational strategies from seeing how other kingdom leaders are pursuing similar work.

Many leaders practice deliberate learning through experience. Some of this approach gets played out in their fields of interest and work. For example, a leader in the field of education may sign up as either a teacher or a learner in a different educational institution or environment. Other leaders seek experiences that serve simply to expand their horizons or stretch their thinking. Examples include working on a special project (perhaps with an international flavor), taking on a sports challenge (training to run a marathon), creating a memorable event for the community (praying a blessing over the city at the New Year's Eve celebration), or commemorating a personal milestone (going on a safari for a wedding anniversary).

Curiosity may have killed the cat, but it enlivens kingdom collaborators. Their persistent "why?" along with "why not?" and "what if?" disposition keeps them leaning into the future in a learning mode, convinced that turning the world upside down is a job that can't be finished in their lifetime.

JESUS LOVED PARTIES. He performed his first miracle at one (John 2:1-11). Apparently he enjoyed them so much his enemies accused him of being a party animal (Matthew 11:18-19). Several of his greatest stories about God and the kingdom involve parties (the wedding feast, Matthew 22:1-14; the parable of the wise and foolish virgins, Matthew 25:1-13). The father of the prodigal threw a party upon the son's return, something Jesus said occurs in heaven every time a person returns to God (Luke 15:10). In fact, Jesus promised a great feast for the gathered-home family of God to inaugurate the eschaton (Matthew 26:29; Luke 22:14-18). The king of the kingdom seems determined to party!

This characteristic of the kingdom informs the ethos of kingdom leaders. They exude joy because they get to announce good news to people—that God is for them. Far from the stultifying and cloying environment of religion, kingdom leaders create communities of freedom and celebration. They call the party—for life!

This chapter is about a deeper aspect of kingdom leadership than merely enjoying having fun and making fun for the people around them. It discusses the ability of kingdom collaborators to convene people for kingdom purposes in order to address issues that thwart the ability of people to experience life as God intends. For the lives of people to get better in our communities, kingdom leaders need to develop and to exercise this convening power and influence. This chapter focuses on how kingdom collaborators demonstrate this signature theme in their capacity to create and to lead collaborative initiatives that move the needle on big societal issues.

THE POWER TO CONVENE

The Stanford Center on Philanthropy and Civil Society, through its publication, the *Stanford School Innovation Review* (SSIR), has identified three "preconditions" that must exist in any community to make "collective impact" possible. *Collective impact* is a collaborative effort that involves multiple sectors of a community taking aim to improve some aspect of community life or to solve a problem plaguing the community. Through adopting a mutual agenda, sharing key measurements, creating multiple reinforcing activities, ensuring continuous communication, and developing backbone support—five key elements of the collaborative path (called "conditions" by the Stanford School)—the partners can achieve together what none of them could do alone. Not only is collective impact successful in its endeavors, its benefits are longer lasting because of greater community ownership.

According to the Stanford School, the three preconditions are *a sense of urgency, adequate resources,* and *a champion.* Without a sense of urgency, no one comes to the table to work together on solutions for tough issues. Some of my work with community groups involves how to create a sense of urgency that something must be done and must be done *now.* The second precondition, adequate resources, includes money but also people and energy and imagination. The third involves the need for a champion. The champion adopts a cause and is willing to work to build a coalition to create awareness of the need or problem, to devise strategies to address the situation, and to push for the implementation of solutions. Without all three of these preconditions in place, collective impact is not achievable.

I mention the Stanford School research because I have high regard for the insights it has given all of us who work in community development. It has given us a common language, particularly those of us who are determined to move the needle in our community on some societal ill—like literacy, race relations, employment or underemployment, and generational and institutional poverty—seemingly intractable problems that beg for adaptive solutions.

Two additional preconditions seem essential, based on my work in this arena. While these two may have been assumed to be included in the "champion" element of the Stanford School, I think they need to be identified separately because of the importance they play in whether a community can successfully engage in collective impact. These two additional precursors for successful collective impact are *coach* and *convener.*

Coach refers to someone who can help shape the conversations and deliberations involved in creating and sustaining effective collaborative efforts that yield results. This is the role I most often play in my own involvement with community development initiatives. Collaboration requires hard work and calls for a range of competencies that for many leaders aren't second nature. Coaching helps to overcome this fairly widespread deficiency.

For our discussion, I want to focus on *convening*. While kingdom leaders play important roles in every aspect of the pursuit of cross-domain collaborative initiatives—from providing resources to serving as champions—I want to call attention to the power of convening. This is what I mean by "call the party"—the ability of kingdom leaders to put the right people in the room or around the table, leaders who can be effective players in surfacing a problem, devising solutions, and creating a coalition committed to addressing the issue.

A couple of examples from my own experience shed light on the power of convening. The impetus for Redwood City's collaborative effort, the Peninsula Literacy Coalition project (PLC), grew out of the minds and hearts of a few kingdom leaders who wanted the church to play its proper role of partnering with God in his kingdom agenda of improving the lives of people in their community.

It just so happened that one of these leaders, John Seybert, had a seat on the city council. John "called a party": two days of critically important interviews that I conducted with government officials, faith-based leaders, school district superintendents and administrators, law enforcement officers, social sector leaders, and local media members. Out of these two days of conversations, these leaders identified literacy as the most critical issue needing to be addressed in their community. Without John's ability to throw the initial party, the PLC would not exist.

Other kingdom leaders stepped up to call parties in their own domains as we moved to the strategy and implementation phase. Over the next eighteen months, they brought together various sectors of the community to focus on literacy. The strategy they developed didn't involve forming a new literacy effort or organization that would be perceived as a competitor by groups already operating in that space. Instead, they opted for creating an effort designed to strengthen and improve the work underway by building closer ties between the community and its schools.

Three years in now, the PLC occupies a unique and special space in the fabric of the city. "We are able to talk about the more meaningful things that shape healthy community and human relationship," wrote Dan Parodi, one of the twin local architects of the PLC.

Gary Gaddini, the other architect, commented recently on the effectiveness of the project:

We have been able to *call the party* [emphasis added] with "tribal leaders" in our city from various domains to discuss what we are going to do in aligning ourselves around literacy. In my highlight with the PLC we had a "night of champions" with the Mayor, Vice Mayor, Police Captain (representing the Chief), Fire Chief, school principals, the Superintendent of RWC Schools, key pastors, and key business people. We provided topnotch desserts and wine and spent 20 minutes defining the problem and then the discussion took off regarding what we can do collaboratively about this.

A second example of the need for a convener comes from an experience in my own hometown, Columbia, South Carolina. In 2012, a group of us developed the vision for a co-ordinated event in which the citizens of our city would engage in community service across all kinds of issues and arenas (beautification, neighborhood revitalization, home construction and repair, education, healthcare, hunger, etc.). Our idea turned into a project called One Columbia: CityServe 2013.

The event was successful, yielding significant community involvement. During the week starting on April 20, 2013, we were able to identify that over 125 projects were undertaken, engaging over 3,000 volunteers in more than 23,000 hours of community service. (We also know that many more dozens of projects, multiple hundreds of volunteers, and thousands of community service hours went unreported.)

How did an idea hatched over a dining-room table grow to such proportions? Because Mayor Steve Benjamin called the party by issuing the invitations to people to serve on the steering committee. In the first meeting of this group (chosen from all sectors of our city), the mayor quoted two Old Testament prophets as he asked people to work and to pray for our city. The mayor's interest in the project signaled to the gathered leaders the importance of their engagement and ensured its success.

We also learned through One Columbia: CityServe the value and importance of an ongoing champion (or champions). No one stepped forward after the event to build on its initial success. The hoped-for annual emphasis hasn't materialized. However, several organizations in our city (most notably the University of South Carolina) have stepped up their community service engagement.

In both of these instances, most of the effort expended was carried out by sectors of the community other than the faith-based domain (though they participated). However, both initiatives grew out of kingdom aspirations. Their impact proves the power of the kingdom to reach across all areas of our communities. They demonstrate that people from all walks of life act as co-conspirators with God's kingdom agenda, even if they're unaware that they're doing so. And both community initiatives show the incredibly important role of kingdom leaders in calling the party. When wielded, that power turns aspirations into results in the lives of real people being better able to experience the life God intends for them.

BUILDING COLLABORATIVE INTELLIGENCE

Once the party commences, a new element comes into play: adaptive solutioning for complex and vexing societal issues requires collaboration. Meaningful community development typically requires cross-domain and intra-domain collaboration between leaders and organizations. This means leaders need to develop their collaborative intelligence.

Genuine collaboration goes way beyond coordination or cooperation. It involves multiple parties setting a common agenda, figuring out success criteria, devising and implementing strategies, measuring success, capturing what is learned, and building a framework of processes that promote the sustainability of the initiatives. The energy to do this derives from the conviction that collaboration yields greater results than siloed efforts.

Many leaders admit that collaboration isn't a skill they were led to acquire. Leaders study a multitude of topics like visioning, persuading, inspiring, managing projects and people and organizations, and strategizing. Collaborating with others to accomplish goals? Not so much.

Here are six foundational understandings a leader must embrace to raise his collaborative intelligence.

1. Influence (leadership) is personal, not just positional. Leaders used to command influence simply by virtue of their job title or managerial position or status in a system. In a network world, collaborative efforts frequently reach across multiple organizational systems and company cultures to yoke people together on tasks and projects who may not care about or even be aware of an individual's status in her own organization or culture. In addition, people are often recruited into collaborative initiatives based as much on preexisting relationships as on their official roles or job titles.

All this means that the effectiveness of collaborative leadership involves managing and nurturing relationships. This capacity to get along can determine if a leader can pull people together to accomplish common goals. This dynamic especially holds true when people working together aren't connected through organizational charts or supervisory lines of authority, but rather through the willingness of people to work with each other. This reality also suggests that the person who provides the emotional glue for a group may not have the highest-ranking job in the company, but provides the chemistry needed to facilitate collaboration. This function—providing emotional Velcro for collaborative teams and efforts—can be a pivotal and strategic role for kingdom leaders to assume.

2. Trust is the currency of collaboration. This dictates that relationships be treated with care and that an atmosphere of respect be cultivated and nurtured. Leaders must promote and practice mutual accountability for all team members, including themselves. Team members must follow through with assignments or promised action. If trust somehow gets ruptured, the team must move quickly to restore it, beginning with admission of fault followed by any restorative action necessary. It can (and often does) take months to build trust; however, the account can be wiped out very quickly, sometimes in one irresponsible act. Trust can also be eroded slowly over time with missed assignments or late performance. To guard against trust corrosion, expectations of and between team members must be clearly stated and understood, then honored.

3. Communication is the lifeblood of collaborative efforts. I find it remarkable that, in a day when we're all bombarded by information, an almost universal complaint I hear in my consulting work with organizations comes from people who say, "Nobody knows what's going on around here!" When I report this to organizational leaders, I can almost see the steam coming out of their ears as they tell me the amount of effort they expend in communicating. I tell them that a common malady of corporate life is that people are so awash in information they become desensitized to communication.

People who collaborate effectively establish communication protocols so that the team stays informed. And collaborative efforts that seek to inform others outside the team have to continue to come up with novel ways to communicate so their voices rise above the sea of information people are drowning in. (One group working to reduce sex trafficking in the United Kingdom placed its ads on coasters in the pubs.) As a rule, *over*communicate. Peter Drucker observed that at the point the leader is sick of hearing himself deliver his message, other people are just beginning to hear it.

4. Roadblocks to collaboration must be addressed. As we've already noted, these roadblocks can form from a breakdown in trust and communication. The causes can be personal, between team players. They can be created by personality clashes or deep character flaws, like leaders' egos that get in the way. A toxic need for control also squelches collaboration. The need to be the hero can make collaboration more difficult as people vie for credit.

Sometimes roadblocks arise from more systemic issues, like the clash of values (particularly troublesome if the misalignment reflects incompatibility between corporate partners who are teamed together). Roadblocks can also be attitudinal, like the "it has to be invented here" perspective that hinders teams and organizations from learning from what others are doing or have done in the same arena.

5. Focus on purpose. Mission serves as the motivator that binds collaborators together. In many ways, purpose is the invisible leader of your team. The ability to form partnerships during challenges that could discourage or even to derail such partnerships lies in the clarity of the group's shared *why*, not the *how*. Purpose leads more through inspiration than through control and structure. Flexibility around methods and tactical approaches is essential in collaborative initiatives. However, fuzziness about the mission often proves fatal.

6. Remember the three Ps: patience, persistence, and perseverance. Collaboration is hard. If that weren't so, everyone would be doing it. Collaborating usually takes longer than anticipated. This can prove discouraging or even defeating to a leader who has great passion to see something accomplished but who begins to wonder if an effort will ever yield results or even begin. Too many leaders give up too soon, often because no one prepared them for this reality. Leaders need to access a reservoir of patience ("this setback is temporary"), persistence ("we're making progress"), and perseverance ("we're not giving up!") to sustain them and their partners. Kingdom leaders can be particularly subject to discouragement because they often are working in arenas that are challenging to begin with. Their disappointment is amplified by a deferred or shattered hope that things should, could, and will get better.

The reward is worth the wait! Some years ago, Tracey Beal brought a team to one of our City Impact Leadership Community cohorts in Dallas. Our process helped her articulate a vision of what she wanted to see happen in her state of Arizona. She envisioned the faith community and business sector serving the public schools in their communities to better support the education of students. She formed School Connect as a statewide effort. For a couple of years, Tracey kept making her pitch to anyone who would listen. She often felt she was making little headway. But others and I kept encouraging her not to give up.

Tracey didn't. And because she didn't, on October 1, 2016, over ten thousand volunteers served 265 schools in thirty school districts on "Love Our Schools" day. School Connect is taking flight! I heard from her just today; she detailed her upcoming School Connect Summit to be held at and hosted by Grand Canyon University. More than thirty superintendents of education are bringing tables of community partners to talk together about collaborating through strategic engagement in their districts. Tracey wrote, "Amazing miracles are happening right and left. Churches, government, business, and nonprofits are all working together to transform schools!" This is all because kingdom leader Tracey called the party—and kept calling—building relationships, establishing trust, honing the message, confronting roadblocks, and just hanging in there when she was tempted to quit.

SO, YOU WANT TO PARTY?

Do you want to be a kingdom leader who can call the party? How do you position yourself to fulfill this role? Here are a couple of suggestions.

Show up at other people's parties. Randy felt called to move back to his home neighborhood. He had a desire to serve the city with its many challenges. Over the years, its economic engine had severely contracted. Businesses had shuttered, a once-vibrant urban center had declined, people had moved out in search of jobs, and those who remained were increasingly in need of help and social services. Randy's old neighborhood in the inner city had degenerated into a high-crime, low-income section of town. He dreamed of being an agent of blessing, being used by God to make life better for the people of the city.

Randy began by showing up at meetings. He went to school board meetings, city council meetings, neighborhood association meetings, clergy prayer meetings, all kinds of meetings. He kept this up for months, always engaging officials and other attendees in conversations about what improvements needed to be made. He didn't offer solutions; he was on a listening and learning mission. He also volunteered to help on projects where he could make a contribution.

After some months of showing up at meetings and volunteering his help, people began to ask *him* questions about his interests and his perspectives on issues. By then Randy had gathered around him a group of like-minded and like-hearted people who were ready to spring into service. Today, some five years later, Randy and his team are significantly engaged in the school district by providing scores of mentors. They serve the arts community with a studio. They act as the volunteer workforce for several festivals and sponsor block parties in conjunction with the police department to build better police-community relationships.

Have I mentioned that Randy is a kingdom-minded Jesus-follower? In addition to all his community engagement, he oversees a network of house churches throughout the city and has regular meetings and dialogues with spiritual leaders across the ethnic and religious spectrum. On multiple occasions, Randy's network of house churches has banded together to serve religious refugees and the Muslim community. These interactions have generated lots of spiritual conversations and exchanges.

None of this would have happened if Randy hadn't attended other people's parties.

Be a boundary spanner. Before the advent of the network world, leaders learned how to function successfully within the boxes and lines detailed in their organizational charts. But the world isn't like that anymore. The fluidity of information, people, and resources across organizational and sectors (domains) requires the presence of people who facilitate connections between various players and organizations. Sociologists and experts in organizational systems have created a term for people who do this: boundary spanners. They have a critical function in an increasingly collaborative world of networked organizations.

In the business world, boundary spanning capabilities are driven by diversity, globalization, technology, cross-sector partnership, and collaborative work both inside and between organizations. Boundary spanning allows businesses to gain knowledge from sources outside their organization. This can take a formal path of mergers and acquisitions or of forming joint ventures, along with more informal pathways of sharing knowledge or engaging in collaborative initiatives with other organizations. Innovative companies and organizations intentionally develop leaders and corporate cultures to support boundary spanning.

Kingdom leaders automatically search for ways to bridge the work they're connected to with the work God is doing in other organizations and sectors. For instance, if you're a kingdom leader with a congregational responsibility, you seek to inform your congregational efforts with what's going on *outside* the church. As a boundary spanner, you look at your ministry with an external lens rather than allowing only internal knowledge and needs to inform your ministry strategies. You introduce the church to external forces at work in the community through a variety of means. Conversely, if you're serving outside the faith community (business, healthcare, education, government, etc.), you look for ways kingdom perspectives and initiatives can become part of your work.

Ron Hogue's work with "beyond-profit" companies demonstrates boundary spanning with a kingdom agenda. Here's how he describes what he does, along with an example of what happens as a result:

I discovered that people in general, businesspeople more specifically, want to know that their work means something. Life is more than a paycheck. It's about leaving a mark on humanity that is unique to you. I present that opportunity to business owners so they can look beyond their businesses, their bank accounts, and P&Ls to the things that give life meaning—people. I bridge these owners with places of unique need so they can own the needs of a group of people and transform the lives of those people forever. It's becoming a beyond profit company. A beyond profit company is a company that extends its profits beyond itself to the needs of others and beyond time into the future.

The present company I'm working with is transforming a group of people who live on a volcanic island surrounded by Nile crocodiles and hippos. They have no food except the fish they catch (which is about one or two a week to feed their families). They have no clean water, no toilets, no commerce, no help from anyone. In fact, the nickname they gave themselves is "the forgotten people." The business owner has funded our ability to give mosquito nets to an island of 2,000 people who were seeing thirty new cases of malaria a month. Now they are down to one or two cases a month. They have built toilets for the people. They had no place to relieve themselves except in the lake. We created seven clean water stations where lake water is brought and filtered. This has almost wiped out the intestinal problems and diseases on the island. We provided professional fishing nets so they could catch fish not only to eat, but also to sell at a local market so they could buy vegetables to eat.

Beyond that, we support a church planter who is starting a church on the island and is supported by a chicken farm we supplied him with. Over 300 people have received Christ. We built an outdoor tabernacle for the people to worship under.

We're not done. We will be doing aquaponic gardens on the island, providing solar lights, shoes for the children, and agribusinesses like chicken and goat farms. What was a place of desperation has been transformed into a place of hope for future generations. All because one company chose to intervene in the lives of those who were orphaned and needed a champion.

Ron is not the only boundary spanner in this story. The business owner who has engaged his services is performing the same function.

What boundary do you face? Is it an internal structural one in your place of work (church or otherwise)? Is it geographical (neighborhood or location) or demographic (age/gender/ethnic)? The truth is, all of us are positioned along some boundary, some horizon between two or more elements. It could be as simple as the boundary between help and need. Kingdom leaders find ways to span two worlds.

Showing up at other people's parties and acting as a boundary spanner requires a kingdom disposition. We have to believe that God is at work in other people (he didn't just show up when we arrived on the scene). We also have to be committed to cultivating a broad bandwidth of relationships, not just practice tribalism, especially when it comes to faith expression. If the kingdom involves helping people experience the life God intends for them, it calls us out to play with others.

When we span boundaries, we're following our master teacher. Think about all the boundaries Jesus spanned. He intentionally went through Samaria, where he reached across ethnic, religious, and gender boundaries to bring the kingdom to bear (John 4). He healed a Roman centurion's servant, then pointed to the Gentile's faith as an example to follow (Luke 7:1-10). He made the point in his hometown sermon in Nazareth that the prophets Elijah and Elisha had reached across boundaries in their day to help the widow in Zarephath and heal Naaman the Syrian (Luke 4:24-30). Jesus called a party at the home of the despised tax collector Zacchaeus (Luke 19:1-9) as well as attending a party thrown by Simon the Pharisee (Luke 7:36-50), where Jesus accepted the lavish offering of a prostitute. Of course, the biggest boundary span he made was bridging heaven and earth! Jesus' life and ministry shattered boundaries and called the party for all who will come.

Today's kingdom leaders do the same.

> SHOWING UP AT OTHER PEOPLE'S PARTIES AND ACTING AS A BOUNDARY SPANNER REQUIRES A KINGDOM DISPOSITION.

PASSOVER WAS A TIME OF celebration for Israel. This feast gave participants an opportunity to pull away from the challenges of everyday life to spend time with family and to revel in gratitude, all laced with historical and spiritual overtones—kind of like our Thanksgiving on steroids.

Jesus made secret arrangements to secure a secluded room for the feast. He wanted to make sure this special time with his supporters wouldn't be disturbed by an interruption, especially by a hostile intrusion.

Preparations had been made. Good food. Good wine. Good conversation. After all, they had been together for the better part of three years. They had seen everything from the calming of life-threatening storms at sea to the resurrection of the dead at a friend's house. From the street riots and cleansing of the temple just days earlier, as well as from the intelligence they were gathering from the crowds, the disciples knew that the situation was growing more dangerous day by day. But that night, in a secluded and secret upper room, it was time to party.

By all accounts, the meal went off without a hitch—except for the embarrassing and hasty departure of Judas. Things didn't get serious until after the bulk of the ritual meal had been navigated. Jesus surely would have enjoyed the laughter and good-natured back-and-forth among the assembled. Yet it's not much of a stretch to think that he probably remained pensive during the revelry. Imagine the confluence of thoughts and emotions he was experiencing. He knew that forces were already in motion for his final and climactic hours on earth.

When Jesus began to speak, he seemed to have another banquet scene in mind—a scene from the future, yet one that was so certain and concrete in his mind that it seemed a mere moment away.

> "I have eagerly desired to eat this Passover with you before I suffer. For I tell you, I will not eat it again until it finds fulfillment in the kingdom of God."
>
> After taking the cup, he gave thanks and said, "Take this and divide it among you. For I tell you I will not drink again of the fruit of the vine until the kingdom of God comes." (Luke 22:15-18)

That vision of the kingdom seemed to have sustained Jesus in the moment. He could see through this world to the next. Not a shadow of doubt entered his mind or heart concerning the reality of the coming kingdom—and that his friends would join him there.

That grand vision inspired hope. But Jesus looked at it through a veil of tears. He knew of impending sorrow and separation even then bearing down on this celebration. The optimism of the king was pain tinged.

This episode in Jesus' final hours reflects a reality that all kingdom leaders learn to live with. Their vision of the kingdom gifts them with optimism. They know that lives will be better off because of the impact of the kingdom. They see all the way through the present world to one that is much better off. But it's a pain-tinged optimism. The vision, after all, is looking through *this* world, where things aren't the way they should be. Where too much injustice occurs. Where too many suffer from too many ravages of the effects and the damage exacted by the dark kingdom of anti-life.

This reality, along with the stresses of serving and leading, takes its toll on kingdom leaders. It is a toll that can touch leaders' spiritual, mental, emotional, and physical health. In the end, kingdom leaders who learn how to navigate the rapids of the colliding dynamics of hope and despair are the ones who finish well. This is the topic for discussion in this chapter. Our investigation will first survey the forces of burnout and compassion fatigue, two dynamics that especially threaten kingdom leaders. Then we'll see how kingdom leaders can build resiliency, the quality that allows them to maintain hope amid their pain.

EFFECTIVE KINGDOM LEADERS LEARN HOW TO SPOT BURNOUT AND DEFEND AGAINST IT.

BATTLING BURNOUT

As noted above, kingdom leaders can be subject to two major derailing forces: burnout and compassion fatigue.

These two conditions differ but can be experienced at the same time. Some leaders experiencing one or the other or both can be confused as to which they suffer from. Whereas compassion fatigue is associated with trauma, burnout is *not* trauma-related. Burnout results from the exhaustion caused by intense or increased workloads and prolonged stress.

Kingdom leaders often wander into or live in these dangerous circumstances. Most problems they take on or issues they pursue clamor for all the attention and time they can give. Combined with the leader's passion to make people's lives better, these prolonged pressures can create an environment where factors conspire to consume all the leader's energy. Effective kingdom leaders learn how to spot burnout and defend against it.

Signs. Psychologist Herbert Freudenberger generally gets credited for the development of the term *burnout*. He identified a number of signs that can signal that a person is experiencing burnout. We all experience some of these signs from time to time. However, should multiple signs begin to become evident in a leader's life, a closer assessment may be called for to determine whether the leader is in burnout mode. The signs to watch for include the following:

▼ *Exhaustion.* Lack of energy associated with feelings of tiredness and trouble keeping up with usual activities.

▼ *Detachment.* People headed for burnout begin putting distance between themselves and others.

▼ *Boredom and cynicism.* The burnout victim begins to question the value of friendships and activities, sometimes even life itself.

▼ *Increased impatience and irritability.* The ability to do things quickly diminishes, and the person begins to blame family and co-workers for things that are his or her fault.

▼ *A sense of omnipotence.* Some victims begin thinking that no one else can do their jobs as well.

▼ *Feelings of not being appreciated.* Burnout victims want to be appreciated for their added efforts, which really aren't producing more, but less. These feelings result in the victim becoming bitter, angry, and resentful.

▼ *Change of work style.* Reduced results and conflicts with others eventually cause burnout victims to withdraw from decisive leadership and work habits.

▼ *Paranoia.* Long-term burnout can lead victims to believe that someone is out to get them.

▼ *Disorientation.* Long-term burnout causes the victim's thoughts to wander, speech patterns to falter and concentration spans to become limited.

▼ *Psychosomatic complaints.* Physical ailments such as headaches, lingering colds, backaches, and similar complaints flourish in burnout victims.

▼ *Depression.* The depression is usually temporary, specific, and localized to one area of life.

▼ *Suicidal thoughts.* Some people may make suicide threats or gestures that are manipulative.

Self-inflicted wounds. Leaders can find themselves in toxic environments that place them at a high risk for burnout.

Almost every workplace and work situation at one time or another can involve periods of high stress. The key word here is *toxic*. In these unhealthy cases, the prudent move is to protect and defend yourself and to look for an emotionally and psychologically healthier environment if the current surroundings can't be changed. The leader has to make the call to bail and when to bail.

Much burnout results from forces and choices *inside* the leader that set him up for burnout. Leaders are often complicit in their exhaustion. Some of the leading causes include the following:

▼ *Approval addiction.* Many leaders have such high needs for approval they fail to maintain appropriate boundaries, allowing others to crowd their personal time and family time. They're reluctant to say no, fearing that others won't like them.

▼ *Achievement/performance standard.* Many leaders feel the need to achieve to win approval—from others as well as from themselves. They may also feel a need to work for God, earning his love by their superhero efforts. Super-achievers also sometimes suffer from the "what's next?" syndrome, having to top their last performance. Highly successful people, if they're trying to fill a hole in their sense of self, are sometimes lulled into believing that the next project or next success will make everything quiet down in their spirit and calm the beast that pushes them from within. When perfect performance is expected in order to win approval of others or in order to meet one's own internal expectations, the leader is operating with perfectionism. Burnout is not far behind when perfectionism keeps them on the ropes of performance anxiety all the time.

▼ *Working outside our strengths.* Much ministry burnout affects leaders dealing with prolonged trivia. What they consider trivia is related to their sense of mission and their talent set. If a leader pays too much rent—that is, does things that are of little interest to him or things that sap his energy—he is a candidate for burnout, especially if this happens over a prolonged period.

▼ *No margins.* Modern life has reached such a complicated level that many leaders operate with no margins in their lives, whether financial, time, energy, physical, or spiritual. The leader who consistently violates the need for some rest—for physical or spiritual replenishment—will automatically court burnout. Often frenetic activity is a form of denial, substituting busyness for intentionality.

Some dance steps to learn. When, as a young teenager, I decided to attend a school-sponsored dance, I asked my older brother to teach me three dance moves I could rely on to get me through the evening. If you're susceptible to burnout, you'll probably dance with it more than once in a lifetime. The dynamics that lead to burnout often can be operating at a very deep—maybe even subconscious—level in the leader. This makes it easier for situations to trigger the onset of the condition. If you suspect you're in this category of increased risk, you'll need to learn these dance steps—and revisit them frequently to maintain vigilance against this destructive enemy of your life and leadership:

▼ *Analyze the true source of your burnout.* Before blaming the job or other people or the Lord, ask yourself the hard questions. What do you do to set yourself up for burnout? Are some of the tendencies above true for you? What repair work do you need to do in your own soul in terms of your sense of self-worth and other areas? Self-awareness is critical.

▼ *Sabbath.* The need for rest involves much more than a change of schedule. A sabbath is intentional time spent with God, allowing him to coach you in your own life development. A sabbath well spent can remind us of who we are and whose we are. Sabbath time also allows God to challenge our freneticism and to remind us that the backdrop of our lives is eternity. We don't have to live to the beat of a tyrannous drum.

▼ *Reassess and reassert your values.* Whatever you say your values are may be a clue to what they are, but how you spend your time and energy is a dead giveaway. If you say that family is a value to you, yet you sacrifice family to meet someone else's needs (maybe your own), then family may not be a value after all. This is a time for honesty and courage as you admit to yourself what really is important to you and then live consonant with those values.

▼ *Spend time with people who give you energy.* This would include family and friends. Many leaders comment that they're lonely. While leadership is lonely, many leaders make it lonelier than it has to be. Cultivate friendships. This may begin with an admission that there are some things you don't do well or even want to do. Being around people who nurture our souls is critical to spiritual vitality.

▼ *Update your skills.* Keeping sharp prevents being locked in a job or career position that's boring, undesirable, or no longer challenging. Ask yourself, "What else am I good at?" or "Where do I need to improve?"

▼ *Pay attention to your body.* People who are tired simply don't have the emotional or mental reserves necessary for long-term health. This means getting enough rest, exercising, and being smart about nutrition. Sleep deficit is on the rise among Americans. Keeping active physically yields benefits in every area of life. Adhering to a diet of good nutrition can be preventive in terms of disease but also in increasing energy.

▼ *Reinvent yourself.* Every leader needs to reinvent herself about every five to seven years, and sometimes more frequently. This can mean taking on different assignments in your current setting or making a shift in venue altogether.

▼ *Work from strengths.* If burnout can come from working outside our strengths, it makes sense to be sure we keep building those strengths. This doesn't mean we ignore our weaknesses, but we spend time doing what we're good at. Getting better at what we're already good at is our best shot at making a significant contribution.

▼ *Simplify.* This may be the hardest piece of advice for a leader. It takes courage to simplify life around a center that becomes more integrated as time goes on. Most spiritual leaders don't face temptations to do evil or to repudiate the faith. The great temptations are those of being diluted or distracted to the point they miss God's design for their best contribution and personal growth.

How do I know all these? Because I needed to learn them myself. My acquaintance with the dragon of burnout began in my mid-thirties. I was fortunate to figure out what was going on and to make some corrections to recover. Occasionally I have to brush up on some of the dance moves that got me through the experience.

CATCHING ON TO COMPASSION FATIGUE

A few years ago, one of my clients in Pensacola, Florida, hosted a seminar for local pastors, church staff, and the staff of various community helping agencies. The seminar focused on recognizing and dealing with a condition called "compassion fatigue." During the previous year, the area had sustained widespread flooding and its accompanying devastation. The seminar invitees all had served as frontline disaster aid workers during the flood and, by the time of the seminar, had been involved in helping displaced and devastated people and families for months. The local hospital— the ones resourcing the seminar event with speakers—had identified the invited participants to be at risk for the trauma-induced condition.

The hospital team knew what they were talking about. Compassion fatigue first became recognized in the healthcare industry, especially afflicting nurses. The condition, sometimes called "vicarious traumatization" or "secondary traumatization," can afflict those who are exposed to the trauma that others have experienced. By listening (sometime repetitively) to intense stories of trauma, the caregiver can begin to experience the feelings and fears of those they help.

What follows is the diminished capacity of the caregiver to feel and to care for others because the caregiver consciously or unconsciously begins to "check out" emotionally as a defense response. This dynamic occurs over time, typically emerging from the cumulative effect of the caregiver's exposure to others' trauma. Recognizing this potential, the Pensacola hospital decided to offer the seminar about a year into flood relief, since the aid workers had been coping with flood victims' traumas for months.

Since compassion fatigue and burnout share some common manifestations, they can sometimes be confused with each other. Commonalities include emotional, mental, and physical exhaustion, along with increasing disconnection and isolation from others. However, compassion fatigue generally has a faster recovery if recognized early and addressed.

Symptoms. As I've already pointed out, the signs associated with compassion fatigue don't come on overnight. And, as I mentioned when identifying the symptoms associated with burnout, it's important to note that every leader can experience some of these signs from time to time. But if the leader is susceptible due to extended compassion expenditure, he should pay attention when a combination of the following conditions manifest:

▼ emotional, mental, and physical exhaustion

▼ sleep disturbance

▼ cognitive debilitation

▼ behavioral shifts

▼ impaired judgment

▼ depression

▼ morale loss

▼ decline in self-worth

▼ diminished hope

▼ feelings of despair

▼ increased anger

▼ loss of spiritual health

▼ hyper-emotional (typical or ordinary occurrences feel "traumatic")

▼ withdrawal or isolation

Combatting compassion fatigue. Many of the prescriptions for addressing burnout apply to compassion fatigue as well, especially in terms of making sure you're getting adequate rest, exercise, and proper nutrition. In addition to these items, the leader who suspects an onset of compassion fatigue will want to do or understand the following.

▼ *Realize that the condition is not a cause to blame others or yourself.* Don't blame others for your condition; they didn't target you to take you down, nor did they pick you out to make your life miserable. Also, don't blame yourself if you're feeling guilty for feeling less compassion, less empathy, or even hostility toward those you're supposed to be helping. These feelings accompany the condition and are "normal" to the experience.

▼ *Talk with somebody*—preferably someone empathetic and nonjudging, and even better if he or she has a mental health background and understands your condition.

▼ *Change your schedule.* Take some time off; shift your routine. Working harder and longer certainly won't help your recovery.

▼ *Play more.* Develop interests that prove restorative to you physically, mentally, and emotionally. I know leaders who use their days off to catch up on work. Not the right move! Figure out something that's fun—and do more of it.

▼ *Avoid self-medicating* through alcohol, nicotine, or other drugs (either stimulants or downers).

▼ *Pay attention to your own needs.* Doing this is not selfish; it's smart. It's just as okay for your needs to be met as for others to have theirs addressed. Depriving or ignoring yourself will hardly create a greater capacity for extending compassion to others.

▼ *Resist the temptation to do something drastic to regain emotional energy.* Going deeper into debt, starting an illicit relationship, or abruptly changing jobs or your home address will complicate your recovery.

▼ *Identify elements of your caregiving* that contribute to higher stress levels and why they make you more susceptible to compassion fatigue.

The good news is that leaders can recover from compassion fatigue with awareness and proactivity. The situations that produce the condition typically have external origins, raising the odds that nondisruptive personal adjustments can attain results rapidly.

CULTIVATING RESILIENCE TO KEEP HOPE ALIVE

It's not good enough for the leader just to bounce back from compassion fatigue or defend against burnout. Avoiding these potentially derailing conditions must be combined with strategies for moving ahead. Leaders who exhibit a pain-tinged optimism have learned resilience. Resilience is what keeps hope alive.

When we think of biblical characters who proved resilient, our thoughts go to Joseph, Moses, David, Jesus, and Paul, for starters. Each faced enormous challenges. Their lives certainly were not stress-free, nor did they always make the right decisions (with Jesus as the obvious exception). Sometimes their agenda seemed to be a lost cause. Yet through it all, they each emerged as the winners over all the forces arrayed against them and even over the circumstances beyond their immediate sphere of control. We remember and respect them, in part, because of the resilience they displayed.

Let's look at some intentional things that resilient leaders do. Some of these reflect habits of response. Some reveal mental attitudes, while others are actions that resilient leaders have in common.

▼ *Resilient leaders don't expect everything to go smoothly.* They aren't caught off guard by the fact that others don't always agree with them, misconstrue their motives, question their vision, or even work actively against their agenda. These leaders have calibrated their expectations based on the reality that every leader who has made significant contributions has faced considerable opposition and surmounted daunting challenges to their leadership.

▼ *Resilient leaders commit to grow through their experiences*, especially the challenging ones. These leaders feel that each leadership episode holds potential for greater self-awareness, increased wisdom, and deeper spiritual connection with God. They demonstrate the determination to glean the insights of leadership experiences to build their knowledge and to be better prepared for future challenges as well as to take advantage of future opportunities.

▼ *Resilient leaders are grounded in relationships.* Behind every good leader stands a cadre of relationships that provides him an anchor, a refuge, a safe harbor, or whatever the leader needs. Effective and resilient leaders cultivate a rich trove of relationships, from family to friends to mentors to resource people. Typically, these relationships stretch across a variety of sectors from home outward, including faith groups, civic organizations, workplaces, and frequently a rich social network. These people help the leader to process, repair, debrief, decompress, rest, recreate, remember— and forget.

▼ *Resilient leaders maintain perspective.* Tunnel vision can make a crisis seem like the end of the world. Effective leaders maintain the long-haul view. Though they may be forced to act less optimistically sometimes because of situations and circumstances seen and unforeseen, resilient leaders don't take their eyes off the goal. A delay doesn't spell doom to them. A surprise stab in the back doesn't mean every person with an alternative opinion is a saboteur. Nor does the whole world come to a stop when their will is thwarted.

▼ *Resilient leaders act decisively.* They may also change their minds. But the one thing they don't do is live in a state of perpetual ambiguity. Nor do they waste energy second-guessing their decisions. They attack problems by acting on what they can do, and they don't obsess over what they can't fix. Their proactive approach increases their confidence. They avoid the tentativeness of indecision.

▼ *Resilient leaders manage their worry.* They worry like anyone else; they just don't let worry get the best of them. These leaders tend not to worry alone, since withdrawal can cause them to lose perspective. They go after facts to make sure they're dealing with the right information in their decision making. They pray and meditate to quiet their spirit. In times of heightened anxiety, they maintain positive human contact to guard against the debilitation of isolation.

▼ *Resilient leaders work very hard.* They don't expect to achieve goals and dreams absent the investment of long hours and intense effort. Because these leaders are motivated by what they hope to achieve, many of them are surprised to be called hardworking. Their vision and values align so that they experience less friction as they push hard for what they believe God wants them to accomplish. They ward off the siphoning of their energy and guard against brain drain by minimizing their exposure to negative people.

▼ *Resilient leaders major on "us" not "I."* When things don't go well, these leaders take personal responsibility; when they enjoy success, they point to their team as the reason. Effective leaders don't hesitate to ask for advice and guidance. They create an environment and culture of trust and honesty, so that when they seek counsel, they get good advice, not just endorsements of whatever they're thinking.

▼ *Resilient leaders practice gratitude.* The apostle Paul understood this principle well. In his letter to the Philippians, he declared that he had learned to be content no matter the situation (Philippians 4:11-12). His statement was embedded in a thank-you note that we know as his letter to the Philippian church (Philippians 4:10). Gratitude, the apostle teaches us, is the beginning of contentment. Resilient leaders carry in their spirit a thankfulness that is palpable and experienced by the people in their leadership constellation. They express gratitude to friends, to colleagues, and to God for the opportunity to serve him. Even when pain and sorrow come, these leaders reflect the attitude "I am blessed"— not a sign of pride or boasting, but of humility, reflecting their awareness of God's goodness.

We talked about the amazing ministry of 6 Stones of Euless, Texas, back in chapter two. One of the many things I admire about that ministry is their vision "to be a catalyst of *hope*" (emphasis added). They call their large ministry facility New *Hope* Center (again, my emphasis). At Christmas every year, they're invited into all the school district's elementary campuses to distribute Christmas gifts and to read the Christmas story to hundreds of kids and their families. What do they call this event? "A Night of *Hope*" (you guessed it, my italics).

Hope is powerful. It changes people. It changes communities like Euless. That's why the optimism of kingdom leaders and kingdom ministries is crucial.

Kingdom leaders know that the kingdom triumphs. They don't sweat the outcome of their work or God's activity on planet Earth. The gates of hell will collapse. All that the anti-life kingdom has marred, stolen, broken, and maimed will be reclaimed and restored. Yet even as they live with this knowledge, kingdom leaders also live with the reality that the kingdom has not fully come. Every victory points to ultimate victory; each disappointment reminds kingdom leaders that a gap remains between what will be and what is.

The result of this knowledge and conviction is that kingdom leaders maintain an optimism born of the hope the kingdom affords. But it's a pain-tinged optimism, an awareness that battles remain and that not everyone is experiencing the life God intends for them. This reality spurs an even deeper yearning in kingdom leaders that the good news of the kingdom become more widely proclaimed and demonstrated.

I LOVE THE WORD *accelerate*. First, I enjoy the physical sensation it describes, whether it's my car responding to increased pressure on the gas pedal or a plane hurtling down the runway toward liftoff or a roller-coaster car picking up speed as it heads into the big drop. Second, I like what *accelerate* signals: something already underway is picking up speed. In my work with leaders through the years, I've discovered that often the role I play with them helps them do exactly that: pick up speed. They typically know where they want to go; they just want help to get there faster. My job focuses on making their next steps intentional so they can arrive at their desired destination sooner rather than later. In other words, I help them accelerate their leadership.

My goal in this chapter centers on this same objective with you. You wouldn't still be reading unless you see yourself as a kingdom collaborator. Hopefully our discussion has confirmed your opinion. You've got some ideas of the kingdom contribution(s) you want to make. Hopefully those notions have been confirmed as well. I find that external affirmation of internal dreams typically inspires confidence that, in turn, can accelerate a person's kingdom leadership.

I want to leave you with a few coaching tips—some intentional steps—that can speed up your kingdom impact. I've organized my comments around two categories. The first set of suggestions is for you if you are a leader in church institutional roles. Perhaps you have stewardship of a congregation or a not-for-profit organization or some other leadership assignment in a charitable organization linked to the church.

The second set of tips are for you if you serve as a kingdom collaborator in any of a variety of domains (government, education, healthcare, etc.). You live out your kingdom role largely as a personal expression of your relationship with Jesus. You may or may not have organizational leadership responsibility; nonetheless, you have people in your constellation of influence. And you hope to accelerate the kingdom through your life and leadership.

TIPS FOR CHURCH LEADERS

If you have the job of stewarding a church or church-related organization in North America, this section is for you. You may also want to read this if you're supporting or following a leader who serves in this capacity, because he or she could use your help.

You probably need to shift the culture. You may be looking at making a program tweak to bring your organization into greater alignment with the mission of God in the world. More than likely, you find yourself operating in a church-centric environment. This means the goal, the scorecard, the focus involves advancing the church organizational agenda and is geared to prop up the church-as-institution advance (we went over this in chapter one).

"Seek first the church" is how "seek first the kingdom" has been understood and pursued. The kingdom-centric agenda proves to be a shock to people who earnestly and honestly have equated the church with the kingdom and have understood that obedience to Jesus' command to seek first the kingdom should be demonstrated by building great churches.

A coaching client of mine called as I was writing this chapter to say that his leadership team was struggling with the concepts presented in my book *Kingdom Come.* When presented with the biblical perspective of the primacy of God's kingdom as his mission on planet Earth, many church leaders think I'm arguing that church-as-institution is evil. I am not. What I *am* saying is that we are misaligned in our mission and don't even realize it. Church-as-institution has had centuries to establish itself as the main event and has had cultural support in the form of Western Christendom. Its "why" is misguided and incomplete.

Shifting a culture is difficult, but it can be done. Cultural transformation requires a three-pronged approach. All three elements must be implemented to make the change effective and lasting.

1. You have to change the *storyline*. A different narrative needs to be intentionally shaped and meticulously applied. You as the leader have the task of educating your followers about the kingdom of God. This theme has to

guide sermon content, Web postings, platform discussions, staff dialogue, elder meeting agendas, budget priorities, time expenditures, facility use, personal conversations, prayer meetings—the whole range of church life. You must give careful attention to clarifying the critical role of the church in the kingdom, or your listeners will hear things you are *not* saying and will resist you.

2. You have to change the *scorecard*. Certainly you'll continue to measure participation in church programming and institutional performance. But the scorecard bandwidth will need to be broadened to include community impact and the progress of initiatives you tackle (for example, the number of kids growing more literacy proficient or the number of community service hours performed by your organization's members). A kingdom-centric scorecard will cause a significant reallocation of your resources (prayer, people, time, money, facilities, technology) for external engagement with the community.

3. You have to change the *stewardship* of your organizational leaders. This means that the leadership (yours and that of others) will shift to a kingdom agenda, not just church-as-institution management. Elder meetings will begin with external items. Prayer concerns will include the welfare of the community. Leadership in your organization automatically will enroll leaders into community engagement. Education and increased exposure to community issues will necessarily become part of

leadership recruitment and development. Leaders will be responsible for establishing and nurturing relationships with leaders in the community. Kingdom leadership characteristics (like the ones we've highlighted in this book) will be cultivated and celebrated.

Celebrate the kingdom leaders in your constellation. Be on the lookout especially for kingdom leaders who serve in other domains. Honor government officials and educators who are in the trenches daily, working to improve the life of your city and of the generation to come. Tell the stories of businesspeople who are leading their companies to become "beyond profit" companies or who are creating jobs and engaging in microeconomic development in under-resourced areas and populations. Elevate the role of those who are befriending their neighbors or starting book clubs or other neighborhood groups where spiritual conversations can take place. Display the work of artists who explore kingdom themes or who galvanize the arts community for altruistic expression. Pray for frontline healthcare workers (and maybe offer a "compassion fatigue" seminar for them). Extol the efforts of those serving in other community social agencies and not-for-profits (and recruit for their campaigns). Perhaps you can highlight one leader a week in your worship gatherings as you pray for the welfare of your city.

Search out other kingdom collaborators and network them. Too many leaders—even sometimes those with a kingdom bent—suffer from isolation. Look for other spiritual leaders and community leaders who share your dreams for a better city and better lives for the people in your community. Meet with them on a regular basis. Find ways to join forces. Create on-ramps to their work so people in your organization can connect with them. Share resources. Determine to practice a *with* approach in your organization's engagements, whether it's by inviting neighbors to participate or forming formalized partnerships on joint community initiatives.

Let's admit that sometimes we shrink from collaboration because we don't want others to see our foibles. Sometimes we pull back from collaborating with others because our pride pushes us to be "the one" or "the organization" that gains recognition for helping others. Collaboration can be frustrating at times, and typically it requires more time to accomplish things, but it's more likely to lead to greater success and sustainability in kingdom efforts.

Update the metaphors that govern your leadership narrative. The church-centric agenda has greatly limited the metaphors that govern the function and character of spiritual leadership. Priests, shepherds, teachers, caregivers, prophets—these words pretty much cover most leadership expressions in the spiritual domain. It's time to add to the list some other words, like journalist (finding good kingdom stories and telling them well), community developer, artist, cultural architect, resource maven, futurist, pioneer, explorer—just to name a few to get your juices going. Look at your own strengths, talents, personality, and passion for clues of additional metaphors that can expand and enrich your leadership narrative. (Astronaut, anyone?)

Remember that the kingdom is for you too! God's kingdom designs aren't all "out there." They include you. Your life is as much a part of God's mission on the planet as anyone else's. The biggest billboard positively and powerfully advertising for the kingdom is a filled-full life. As you exhibit vibrancy, resilience, joy, and hope, you help people believe all over again. So look after yourself—emotionally, physically, mentally, and spiritually.

"Imitate me," the apostle Paul said (1 Corinthians 4:16). I don't think this was hubris on his part. I think he was saying, "If you want what I have, then do what I do." As kingdom leaders, we want to be able to say the same thing to our followers, for the same reason.

FOR CHURCH-AS-MOVEMENT LEADERS

If you serve as a kingdom agent in other domains, you face different challenges than do your brothers and sisters who are striving to realign church-as-institution with God's kingdom mission. You know your mission is being played out largely in the world. Your challenge is to align *your life* with it, so that you live every day with an awareness of what God is up to in the people around you and in the situations that you and they face. While you know that the kingdom is alive and well, you yearn for it to be more manifest. For your role in leading the movement in the world, here are a few coaching tips.

See your personal leadership constellation as your first-order mission field for kingdom expression and influence. There's a reason you have your position of leadership. God isn't caught off guard by your leadership; he has put you there deliberately. You may be motivated to tackle some issue in your city or half a world away. Don't ignore that call, but also don't disregard the rich potential to serve the people right around you. The people who follow you constitute a stewardship of opportunity. You have the privilege and responsibility of working to ensure they have a chance to experience the life God intends for them.

This stewardship extends to the spiritual dimension of life, but it includes other aspects: paying attention to work conditions, to team environment, to fair compensation, to personal development opportunities, to mental health support. The leader's exercise of this stewardship is as varied as the leadership assignment.

Network with other kingdom leaders. I think it's important to connect with other Jesus-followers and kingdom agents. First, you can learn a lot from your peers, especially if they're in your industry, about how they're using their influence for kingdom impact. Second, it never hurts to have cheerleaders who are praying for you and providing accountability. Third, these other people need *you* in *their* lives. All these things you need from them are the very elements you provide to them for their own journey.

Make your home a kingdom outpost. The emphasis on leadership in public domains is not meant to suggest that home base isn't important. Please see your home as a critical kingdom incubator. If you have children, it's important to get them thinking from an early age about their own kingdom assignments—how to be good neighbors and friends, the importance of helping and serving others, seeing their lives as blessings. Your children need to be involved in what you are engaged in. Hold intentional dinner conversations around the family dining table to talk about your kingdom perspective and efforts. Actively engage them to serve with you whenever possible.

An increasing number of families are adopting projects and pursuing serving initiatives as a family expression, such as travel to mission sites. Many also see the importance of developing local engagement so that an ongoing missional lifestyle is cultivated in family members. I know one man who heads a not-for-profit who got his first experience in mission work when his high school daughter invited him to accompany her on an overseas missions trip. It changed his life and knitted them very close together as a family team. Another way of positioning your home as a kingdom outpost is to be a hospitality center for the neighborhood. Being a place of warmth and welcome builds a better neighborhood and creates opportunities to engage people in spiritual conversations.

Make your conversations more intentional. Most of us don't need a lot of practice getting better at making small talk about the weather and politics and what we're up to at work. But we could get better at having spiritual conversations. (This serves as an indictment of the church culture for its failure to better prepare us in this regard.) Improving the two skills of active listening (actually paying attention to what people are saying) and asking great questions (probably not starting with "if you died tonight") would yield great dividends in opening up better conversations in general and spiritual conversations in particular.

Practicing spiritual conversations will help you get better at it. Focus on other people (a gift typically not afforded them). Pray that the Spirit will guide you in the conversation. Don't worry about having answers to questions like "why does bad stuff happen?" or "where did God come from?" Many of us in the faith have adopted the idea that we're supposed to be "the answer people." Nothing shuts down a conversation like having all the answers! We don't have to defend the faith; we're just supposed to share it, and only at a conversational speed, not out of compunction to deliver the whole load on the first date.

PEOPLE WILL TELL US WHAT THEY'RE READY FOR— AND WHEN—IF WE LISTEN.

People will tell us what they're ready for— and when—if we listen. We aren't in the selling or telling business; we're just fellow journeyers in life, leaning into others' lives because we want them to have the best life possible—because that's what God wants for them. That's the good news (gospel) of the kingdom!

Get better at becoming you. Don't let the world—or the church acting like it!—squeeze you into its mold. If you don't become *you*, we'll miss *you*, because you're the only *you* we've got. God's mission has *you* squarely in its crosshairs. You were created on purpose for a purpose. Your becoming *you* is his great design for your life. As you determine the contribution you want to make—and make it—your life will be "full-filled" because you are filled full of the life God intends for you.

Fight distraction. Move past disappointment. Realize that discouragement is a tool of your soul's enemy to try to knock you off your game, because nothing threatens him and his kingdom more than a viral kingdom agent. Be that agent!

ACCELERATE THE FUTURE

The kingdom reveals the future. It is God's preferred future for us all. Every time we pray "thy kingdom come" we're pressing the fast-forward button in God's agenda. Our prayer calls for a future not just to come near, but to invade and to change the present. Jesus instructs us to ask that his kingdom show up on earth, in real time, in real people. Each time a life is lifted, a person regains hope, a soul finds its home with God, and the future accelerates. The kingdom comes!

So, buckle in! We're about to accelerate.

I STEPPED ONTO THE hotel elevator along with a mom and her two young sons. The three of them wore wet bathing suits and had towels draped around them. As the elevator made its climb, the mom fished the room key from her pool bag and handed it to the younger boy, who looked to be about four years old. When he took the key from his mom, he jumped up and down, full of the joy that only a small child feels. "It's my turn with the key!" he crowed, as if the chance to slide the piece of plastic through the door lock was like sliding on the green jacket at Augusta National.

When the elevator door opened to their floor, the boy charged off like he was headed to his favorite ride at Disney World. As the door closed, I chuckled at his rapturous thrill.

The episode reminded me of another time when a key was handed out.

When Jesus came to the region of Caesarea Philippi, he asked his disciples, "Who do people say the Son of Man is?"

They replied, "Some say John the Baptist; others say Elijah; and still others, Jeremiah or one of the prophets."

"But what about you?" he asked. "Who do you say I am?"

Simon Peter answered, "You are the Messiah, the Son of the living God."

Jesus replied, "Blessed are you, Simon son of Jonah, for this was not revealed to you by flesh and blood, but by my Father in heaven. And I tell you that you are Peter, and on this rock I will build my church, and the gates of Hades will not overcome it. I will give you the keys of the kingdom of heaven; and whatever you bind on earth will be bound in heaven, and whatever you loose on earth will be loosed in heaven." (Matthew 16:13-19)

When Jesus established his church, he handed out a key to his disciples—not to grant access to a hotel room but to unlock the door between heaven and earth.

Here's an example of what I mean. In early November 2015, I witnessed the birth of a new kingdom initiative. The setting was opening day at the Table Café in the Portland community of Louisville, Kentucky, an underresourced part of that city. The restaurant is the soul child of Church of the Promise, a new congregation in the neighborhood. "We wanted to be an organic expression of church," Pastor Larry Stoess told me. As the church took stock of the community, three issues stood out: food insecurity, the need for employment

WHEN JESUS ESTABLISHED HIS CHURCH, HE HANDED OUT A KEY TO HIS DISCIPLES— NOT TO GRANT ACCESS TO A HOTEL ROOM BUT TO UNLOCK THE DOOR BETWEEN HEAVEN AND EARTH.

opportunities, and the need for job training. How could they address all three? The answer: the Table Café.

The Table is not like most restaurants. Drop in for lunch (for some really good food!), and you'll see what I mean. At the community tables, homeless people sit next to business-people. That dynamic isn't common itself, but when the check comes, it really gets interesting. Some people can't pay; they don't have the money. So they don't, and that's okay. Others pay what they can. That's okay. Some volunteers "pay" by working at the restaurant. That's arranged gladly. If you *do* have the money, you have a couple of options. You can pony up for your meal, or you can "pay it forward" by paying more than your ticket to cover others' meals.

How's all this working? I got the following report from Pastor Larry, who, like most of his congregation, lives in the neighborhood.

In November, we celebrated our first-year anniversary. . . . The benchmarks we set to measure success were blown out of the water.

▼ We needed to serve sixty paying patrons per day to break even—we serve over one hundred patrons daily who pay it forward at an average of 40 percent.

▼ We wanted 20 to 30 percent of our patrons to be "pay with your time" customers—we averaged 28 percent.

▼ We had over nine hundred volunteers over the course of the year.

▼ We wanted to serve five thousand meals; we served eight thousand.

We are making plans now to launch a culinary training program in the summer of 2017 with job placement as the end goal.

Last Friday morning someone paid for every open ticket in the restaurant. The rest of the day everyone who ate at the café paid for the next person's meal. No one paid for their own meal the entire day! Generosity is contagious.

To top it all off, the Table was featured on the Food Network show *Diners, Drive-ins, and Dives.*

Besides reclaiming a decayed corner of shuttered space and turning it into a vibrant hub of positive energy in the community, what has this expression of kingdom done for Church of the Promise (which meets for weekly worship in the back of the building housing the restaurant)? Again, Larry comments:

> The success of the Table has helped deepen the life of our church. We've added to our numbers in a modest way but the best indicator of kingdom growth is the increase in community engagement on multiple levels: people serving at the café, serving at Celebrate Recovery, planning and hosting our weekly community meal, people organically meeting each other's physical and social needs.

Larry and his band of Jesus-followers at Church of the Promise demonstrate what it means to be the people of God partnering with God in his redemptive mission in the world. They are seeking first the kingdom of God. Because they are, life is better in the Portland community—physically, economically, socially, spiritually.

The Table Café is part of something much bigger. It's the reality we know as the kingdom of God. The kingdom is a movement. It changes places—and people. It bridges worlds, shedding some heaven around on earth. It helps us believe that God hasn't given up on us, is still looking for us, and wants all of us to come home.

The movement needs leaders. Leaders who self-select into kingdom leadership by stepping up to the call. Leaders who understand the big picture of what God is up to in the world. Leaders who know how to pray powerfully, agitate effectively for change, combine social and spiritual entrepreneurship, marry vision with action, develop people, curry their curiosity, convene leaders, and convey optimism. These leaders accelerate the coming kingdom.

In the early days of church-as-movement, Paul and Silas journeyed to Thessalonica to preach the good news of Jesus. They enjoyed early success that threatened resident religious leaders, who promptly incited a street riot. The mob dragged some of the new believers to court, charging them with disturbing the peace. In their opening remarks, the plaintiffs characterized the situation as follows: "These who have turned the world upside down have come here too" (Acts 17:6 NKJV).

Kingdom collaborators welcome the accusation. They see it as a badge of honor and wear it proudly.

Grab your badge! It's your turn with the key.

ACKNOWLEDGMENTS

FOR ME THIS SMALL PORTION of text poses a daunting, even fearful, challenge. What if I leave someone out that I should mention? However, it only seems right to acknowledge the people who have inspired this book and brought it to print. And I can remember how I felt when the publisher of a previous book of mine omitted this section inadvertently (I had sent them the text for it). I was devastated that my list of champions went unthanked publicly. So here I go again, gratitude trumping anxiety.

I cannot name the host of kingdom leaders whose lives and leadership have educated me in my engagement with them over the years. The themes that I report on in this volume have not only distinguished their leadership; they have also made the world a better place as they have been practiced. These leaders are helping to bring some of heaven to some of earth. They are not merely reciting the Lord's Prayer as an expression of faith; they are helping to answer it!

Some people who made this book a reality *can* be named. Mark Sweeney, my agent, provides encouragement and insight at every juncture of my writing adventures. We've been at it together for most of two decades now. Somewhere along the way our business relationship gave way to friendship. I'm better off for it! (I started to say "richer for it" but don't want Mark to think I'm holding back on him.)

From my days as a college student I have always admired InterVarsity Press. I remember how excited I would be at receiving their catalog in the mail, then how I would wrestle with my student budget to decide how many and which books I could order, then almost breathlessly unpackaging the procured volumes so that I could tear into reading them. Having the chance now to publish with them is a great honor. I hope I don't diminish the brand! Specific shout-outs go to Helen Lee, who saw the book's potential; Anna Moseley Gissing, my editor, and Amy Spencer, my copyeditor, who helped bring coherence to the manuscript; and Andrew Bronson and his team, who have worked hard to get this book noticed and acquired by you.

I wish everyone had a cheerleader like Cate. She not only inspires me to keep going; she affords me the time and energy to write by magnificently managing much of the chores and functions of hearth and home that provide me a conducive environment and requisite margin to incorporate writing into everything else I do. She cedes blocks of what could be "our time" to this solitary work of writing. It's not just solitary for me; she unselfishly endures her own solitude imposed by this pursuit. "Because," she says, "it matters."

You'll be the judge of that, dear reader! I hope the book is worth it for you and for the people in your constellation of influence as you collaborate with God and others to right an upside-down world.

FOR FURTHER REFLECTION

INTRODUCTION: THY KINGDOM COME

1. What is your own understanding of the kingdom of God?

2. How has this chapter contributed to your understanding of the kingdom?

3. What is the relationship between the church and the kingdom?

CHAPTER ONE: PRAY WITH EYES WIDE OPEN

1. How do you practice listening in prayer?

2. What changes in your prayer life, if any, do you plan to make after reading this chapter?

3. Where do you see God most often?

4. What's new with you? How may God be at work in it?

CHAPTER TWO: FOMENT DISSATISFACTION WITH THE STATUS QUO

1. What wrong or injustice breaks your heart?

2. How are you "selling the problem" to others?

3. How may you address your heart's concern?

CHAPTER THREE: COMBINE SOCIAL AND SPIRITUAL ENTREPRENEURSHIP

1. What characteristics of entrepreneurs do you see operating in your life? Which ones are a harder fit for you?

2. What spiritual or social entrepreneurial projects are you engaged in currently?

3. What projects are you dreaming about?

CHAPTER FOUR: MARRY VISION AND ACTION

1. What would someone who observed you over the past three weeks say your values are?

2. Who needs to join you "at the table" to accelerate your kingdom expression?

3. Think about a positive experience you've had as a volunteer and a negative one. What made the difference between the two experiences?

CHAPTER FIVE: SHAPE A PEOPLE-DEVELOPMENT CULTURE

1. How do you learn best?

2. Which of the core elements of people development do you need to incorporate more into your personal growth?

3. How do you know that you're making progress as a disciple of Jesus?

CHAPTER SIX: CURRY LEADERSHIP CURIOSITY

1. Who or what are you learning the most from?

2. What are you currently exploring?

3. What have you unlearned over the past year?

CHAPTER SEVEN: CALL THE PARTY

1. Which components of collaborative intelligence pose the biggest challenge to your leadership?

2. What parties are you attending that others have called?

3. How are you serving as a boundary spanner?

CHAPTER EIGHT: MAINTAIN (A PAIN-TINGED) OPTIMISM

1. How do you maintain hope?

2. Are you battling burnout or compassion fatigue? What symptoms are manifesting in your life?

3. What suggestions for cultivating resilience do you find most helpful?

CHAPTER NINE: ACCELERATE YOUR IMPACT

1. Which tip for church-as-institution leaders is most helpful/insightful for you? Why?

2. Which tip for church-as-movement is most helpful/insightful for you? Why?

3. What other ideas do you have to accelerate your kingdom leadership?

NOTES

2 FOMENT DISSATISFACTION WITH THE STATUS QUO

34 *People don't buy:* Simon Sinek, "How Great Leaders Inspire Action," TEDx, September 2009, https://www.ted.com/talks/simon_sinek_ how_great_leaders_inspire_action.

3 COMBINE SOCIAL AND SPIRITUAL ENTREPRENEURSHIP

47 *Joey and company approach church planting:* The restaurant is only part of Joey's church planting strategy. Several dozen missional communities have developed in the surrounding neighborhood as another piece of this incarnational kingdom ministry.

62 *There is more than one:* "One College Turns Its Football Field into a Farm and Sees Its Students Transform," PBS NewsHour, September 12, 2016, www.pbs.org/newshour/bb/one-college-turns-football -field-farm-sees-students-transform.

We are now the owner/operator: Email from Tony Johnson to the author, July 7, 2016.

4 MARRY VISION AND ACTION

64 *fifty new cabins:* A unique feature of this housing village is that it's designed for people with criminal records who are battling drug-use issues and mental health challenges. These factors, which typically disqualify a person from being considered a good candidate for housing, serve as the *qualifying* requirements to secure a cabin in the new village. This approach serves as another example of adaptive solutions: the cabins cost less to build than a two-year budget for caring for this population on the street.

74 *Someone will figure out:* "One College Turns Its Football Field into a Farm and Sees Its Students Transform," PBS NewsHour, September

12, 2016, www.pbs.org/newshour/bb/one-college-turns-football
-field-farm-sees-students-transform.

5 SHAPE A PEOPLE-DEVELOPMENT CULTURE

84   *It gave me the opportunity:* Excerpts from student papers provided by
Dave Rocheleau, University of South Carolina, Department of Mechanical Engineering.

7 CALL THE PARTY

117   *Stanford School Innovation Review (SSIR):* I discuss both the preconditions and conditions identified by the Stanford researchers in my
book *Kingdom Come* (Carol Stream, IL: Tyndale, 2015), in the chapter
"When Collaboration Works," 109-32.

120   *We are able to talk about:* Dan Parodi, email to the author, January 10,
2017.

      We have been able to call the party: Gary Gaddini, email to the author,
January 17, 2017.

127   *Amazing miracles are happening:* Tracey Beal, email to the author,
January 10, 2017.

130   *I discovered that people in general:* Ron Hogue, email to the author,
January 10, 2017.

8 MAINTAIN (A PAIN-TINGED) OPTIMISM

137   *Psychologist Herbert Freudenberger generally gets credited:* Freudenberger's seminal work was his book (coauthored with Geraldine
Richelson) *Burnout: The High Cost of High Achievement* (Garden City,
NY: Doubleday, 1980).

CONCLUSION

167   *In November, we celebrated:* Larry Stoess, email to the author, January
2017.

IVP PRAXIS
EQUIPPING LEADERS FOR MINISTRY

God has called us to ministry. But it's not enough to have a vision for ministry if you don't have the practical skills for it. Nor is it enough to do the work of ministry if what you do is headed in the wrong direction. We need both vision *and* expertise for effective ministry. We need *praxis*.

Praxis puts theory into practice. It brings cutting-edge ministry expertise from visionary practitioners. You'll find sound biblical and theological foundations for ministry in the real world, with concrete examples for effective action and pastoral ministry. Praxis books are more than the "how to"—they're also the "why to." And because *being* is every bit as important as *doing*, Praxis attends to the inner life of the leader as well as the outer work of ministry. Feed your soul, and feed your ministry.

If you are called to ministry, you know you can't do it on your own. Let Praxis provide the companions you need to equip God's people for life in the kingdom.

www.ivpress.com/praxis